'I have to believe that this is the most transparent, easy to read, practical self-help book ever written. There is some small piece of hope and wisdom for everyone in this captivating book on the small steps we can take to live a very large life.'

Dr. Kirk Strosahl, co-founder, Acceptance and Commitment Therapy. Author of *In This Moment: Five Steps for Transcending Stress Using Mindfulness and Neuroscience*

'I love this book. It's done the near impossible: it's boiled down solid, evidence-based behavioural principles into a really fun and useful guide for how to shape your own actions and choices in small, steady, do-able increments, in a way that is most meaningful and impactful to you.'

Dr. Lisa W Coyne, Licenced Psychologist & Assistant Professor, Harvard Medical School. Author of *The Joy of Parenting*

'Filled with evidence-based wisdom presented in clear, simple language, this book helps us all take the small steps now that can change the course of our lives. Highly recommended.'

Dr. Steven C. Hayes, co-founder, Acceptance and Commit-ment Therapy. Psychology Professor, University of Nevada, Reno. Author of *Get Out of Your Mind and Into Your Life*

'Some of the most profound realisations are obvious once they are explained. They simply change your life. *The Power of Small* is full of such realisations and life-changing practices.'

Dr. Mary Welford, Consultant Clinical Psychologist, Compassionate Mind Foundation. Author *Compassion-focused Therapy for Dummies*

'*The Power of Small* is the go-to guide if you want to make a positive and sustainable difference to your life. Highly recommended.'

Dr Michael Sinclair, Chartered Psychologist; Director, City Psychology Group. Author of *Mindfulness for Busy People* and *The Little ACT Workbook*

'*The Power of Small* is a game-changer of a book, maybe a life changer, too! The authors will become more than experts to you as you work through their programme, small step by small step. This is powerful, witty and wonderful.'

Dr. Dennis Tirch and Dr. Laura Silberstein-Tirch, Clinical Psychologists, The Centre for Compassion-focused Therapy, NYC. Authors of *The ACT Practitioner's Guide to The Science of Compassion*

The Power of Small

How to Make Tiny But Powerful Changes When Everything Feels Too Much

Aisling and
Trish Leonard-Curtin

HACHETTE
BOOKS
IRELAND

First published in 2019 by Hachette Books Ireland
First published in paperback 2020

Copyright © Aisling and Trish Leonard-Curtin

A CIP catalogue record for this title is available from the British Library.

ISBN 978 1 47366 698 6

Typeset by redrattledesign.com

Printed and bound in Great Britain by Clays Ltd, Elcograf, S.p.A.

Hachette Books Ireland policy is to use papers that are natural, renewable
and recyclable products and made from wood grown in sustainable forests.
The logging and manufacturing processes are expected to conform to the
environmental regulations of the country of origin.

Hachette Books Ireland
8 Castlecourt Centre
Castleknock
Dublin 15, Ireland

A division of Hachette UK Ltd
Carmelite House, 50 Victoria Embankment, EC4Y 0DZ

www.hachettebooksireland.ie

For my Nanny Curtin, for the many, many, many small things that you did for me throughout my life, especially during my adolescence. Your homemade apple tart and brown bread always gave me a sense of connection and peace, even when I was at the heights of anxiety and the depths of grief. I love you and I am so grateful for your presence in my life. ALC

For my dad, who passed away earlier this year. Ever since I can remember he encouraged my insatiable curiosity and appetite for learning, generously nurturing my love of books, nature and music. I feel very blessed to have had his love, support and his consistent belief that I could be whoever I wanted to be and achieve anything I put my mind to. TLC

Contents

Foreword

Reading this book, I found myself saying regularly: 'Gosh! That's me.' It's not always a comfortable feeling to recognise your own fears. Mine is of failure. It is one of the most common self-bullying thoughts we have, say the authors. So they suggest that to stop these thoughts controlling us, we should acknowledge them and then repeat them out loud quickly for 40 seconds. Failure, they say, is a word to which most of us have a visceral response. True. The first time I said it, it really hurt. 40 seconds later it didn't hurt so much. By acknowledging and naming it, I had managed to take some of the harm out of it. It was a small step but a first step, maybe, to dismantling a fear that brings stress and pain to our lives.

Much of this book is about acceptance: 'The more we try to avoid unwanted emotions, the more we are prone to anxiety and depression.' Sometimes we make ourselves too busy, in order to avoid feeling grief. Sometimes we have thoughts of which we are ashamed, like being resentful of a parent with dementia. We should write that feeling of resentment down, say the authors; acknowledge to ourselves privately what we can't say publicly.

This is also a book about getting to know ourselves again. I use a computer every day with powers that weren't even dreamt of when I was born. And yet in this world of great technical complexity, we seem to have become less aware of our own minds and bodies, and less able to be at home with ourselves. Like our iPhones and computers, say Aisling and Trish at the beginning of their book, we are on all the time, and we end up feeling overwhelmed.

The answer doesn't have to be big and dramatic. Small things like walking outside your house in the fresh air for five minutes, or sitting for two minutes quietly breathing, and noticing your breathing, can be powerful. Mindfulness, the authors explain, is also learning not to live life on autopilot, but savouring every moment: listening carefully to friends; listening carefully and completely to music; noticing every bite you are eating; noticing the sounds outside, the wind, the colour of everything.

There are other simple things – like learning to say no. About 15 years ago, I found myself agreeing to do too many things because I find it hard to refuse people. So I put a sticker on my phone which said: 'Just Say No'. It worked. Someone else was always found to do the job and I was less stressed. As the authors say: if you can't say no to people, you just end up being resentful of them.

The aim of this book is to help people live more fulfilling lives, to help them move outside the prisons they have built for themselves. That's the sort of work that Aisling and Trish do every day. They end their book with a poignant quote from Oliver Wendell Holmes: 'Most people die with their music still inside them.'

The Power of Small aims to help us unlock, for ourselves and the world, that wealth of unheard music.

Olivia O'Leary, October 2018

Introduction

A thousand-mile journey
begins with a single step. Lao Tzu

Have you noticed that every second person you're speaking to these days seems overwhelmed? If you're not overwhelmed in your work life, chances are you're overwhelmed in your personal life. Never before have we been expected to be on in so many different contexts, and on an ongoing basis. It can feel like the goalposts are always shifting. We're being asked to do and be more and more with less and less time, energy and resources.

There are small, yet effective, tools and strategies that can help you break down any overwhelming situation and decipher what would be the most effective action you can take at this particular moment in time – and that is what the journey of this book is about.

We are psychologists who also happen to be a married couple. Our collective aim in writing this book is to teach you the smallest skills, which will result in the maximum positive impact on your life.

We have both experienced mental health difficulties and overwhelming life challenges. Our training has equipped us with the tools to shape our knowledge and experience into the concepts enshrined in the Power of Small. But we do not approach this solely from the position of professional qualification and experience. We have brought to the development of the Small concept our joint lived experience. Where useful, we will bring elements of these personal experiences to bear during the course of the book – both their detail, and how we have been helped by the application of the Power of Small to situations we have faced.

We believe that our past experiences coupled with our psychological knowledge of evidence-based compassionate strategies will allow us to give you a small skills kit full of small, yet powerful, tools for even the most difficult of life circumstances.

What the Power of Small is, and how it works

People who come to see either of us individually or to attend one of our groups, generally are not in a great place in their lives. They are often burdened by a long list of all the things they believe are wrong with them, others and the world. Of course, they have an equally long list of what they want us to help fix.

When someone comes to see us in a state of distress, we can more often than not tell where the central problem lies pretty quickly. Through asking a few key questions, we can pinpoint what areas of their life are on track and which ones have gone off course.

Big promises, big disappointment

A client called Michelle comes to see us. She is unhappy in her relationships, and is suffering both physically and psychologically. She absolutely hates her job and can't even remember the last time she had spontaneous fun. Much of the time, her life barely feels worth getting out of bed for.

Michelle wants big changes, and she wants them fast. However, if she gets overly caught up in trying to change everything all at once, she is likely to find herself paralysed from simply moving forward at all.

Michelle has got caught up in this trap of big promises, big disappointment many times before. She has spent thousands of euros and countless hours investing in the latest quick-fix solutions. She invariably starts off all guns blazing, but then quickly crashes and burns. She has gradually become more and more disillusioned, and over time has concluded that her life is unchangeable.

Michelle has been disempowered by always thinking too big. Our job is to help her change her life by thinking in small, incremental steps – and this way laying the foundations and building blocks for sustainable, long-lasting change.

The most effective way to achieve this is to break

everything down into small, manageable steps, rather than resorting to quick fixes. Quick fixes may lead to short-term gain, but in the long-run they result in continued pain.

This book is all about giving you the skills to break everything down into small steps, in a manageable way. This may involve you sometimes experiencing short-term pain. However, from our experience, and the experiences of those we have worked with, the long term gain will be more than worth it. Having said that, it is important to add that the small journey often contains twists and turns, and requires an ongoing commitment to the principles in order to achieve the maximum impact.

In this book we've broken down the many life-saving and life-enhancing skills we have learned into small, easily digestible chunks, which you can use one at a time, slowly building momentum to achieve the big changes you want in a gradual, yet sustainable, way.

We give clients like Michelle just one thing to do after each session that will take five to ten minutes per day. There may be supplementary reading or exercises we recommend, but the core action that will help Michelle the most is so short and manageable that she will likely engage in it, and it will lead to positive change.

Similarly, in this book we will be recommending small actions at the end of each chapter.

The book is divided into four parts. Part One will help you identify your comfort zone, and also the actions you take – actions that are motivated by a desire to move towards a more fulfilling life, and those that are motivated by a desire to control or avoid unwanted experiences. Part Two will help you identify what needs to change in order to live a more purposeful and meaningful life.

We will provide you with a Power of Small toolkit in Part Three. Here we will share key skills and strategies to show you how to change your current unhelpful responses to being overwhelmed. In Part Four we will give you some small takeaways – nuggets of wisdom, tips and tools to maintain the gains you will have achieved through utilising the Power of Small.

By the end of the book, if you engage in this process by following through one tiny action at a time, you will have a kit full of effective tools that can be applied to even the most overwhelming of situations. This is a kit that you can come back to whenever life feels like it's too much. You'll be able to choose which skills you need to refresh to best enable you to make tiny but powerful changes.

TODAY'S SMALL STEP

Your small steps diary

Get a journal and on the first page write, 'My Small Steps Diary'. This is where you will record your Power of Small journey as you work through this book. You can purchase a notebook that is really appealing to you, or if that feels like too much, you can maybe use a copybook or journal you already own.

Your small steps diary will be something you can come back to whenever you feel overwhelmed. If you engage with this book fully, your diary will contain a great number of personalised skills, tools and strategies that you will have developed bit by bit.

The Small Basics
Limbering Up for Life

*There is something wonderfully bold and liberating
about saying yes to our entire imperfect
and messy life.* Tara Brach

The Power of Small is grounded in the tenets of Acceptance and Commitment Therapy (ACT), which was developed in the US by psychologists Dr Steve Hayes, Dr Kirk Strosahl and Dr Kelly Wilson.

ACT is an effective approach to helping people with a wide range of issues, from depression and anxiety, to chronic pain and addictions. It is helpful for those experiencing workplace burnout or those wanting to increase their productivity and leadership skills. It has also been hugely beneficial for athletes wanting to hone their sporting abilities.

The premise behind ACT is that you are most likely to struggle and suffer when you are being *psychologically inflexible*. Every single one of us falls into the psychological inflexibility trap from time to time; it is a totally normal response to the often overwhelming world we live in. The aim of ACT is to help you become more psychologically flexible.

What is psychological flexibility?

While physical flexibility is your ability to bend, move and respond to whatever is going on in your physical environment, on the other hand psychological flexibility is your ability to stay grounded in the present moment, even when distressing events occur. It's about staying connected to what matters to you most, letting your values guide your actions rather than being pushed around by unwanted thoughts and emotions.

Just as you can learn to become more physically flexible through activities such as stretching, exercising and eating healthily, you can also learn how to become more psychologically flexible through practising reflection and mindfulness, for example, and doing things that bring long term gain, even when they are uncomfortable.

And just as there are actions that lead to greater physical inflexibility, such as living a sedentary lifestyle with little exercise, there are also actions that result in a person being more psychologically inflexible. Psychological inflexibility has been shown to increase the risk of depression, anxiety, addictions, disorders and general dissatisfaction with life.

Three states of mind that lead to psychological inflexibility

1. **Lack of awareness in the present moment**
   When you are preoccupied with the past or future, you become psychologically inflexible. Because you are either rehashing what has happened already, or becoming entangled in what may or may not happen, you lose contact with the only time when you can actually influence the course of your life – the present moment, right here and now.

2. **Getting caught in thinking and emotional traps**
   This is when you either get blinkered by your thoughts and emotions, to the extent that you lose contact with the present moment, or when you get caught in a vicious cycle of pouring all of your time and energy into futile attempts *not* to think a particular thought or feel a particular feeling. These traps usually result in your engaging in actions that feel good in the short term, yet carry a heavy long term price tag.

3. **Disengagement from what really matters**
   Whenever your actions lack a sense of direction, purpose or authenticity, you will likely become more psychologically inflexible. When you are unclear about what is important to you, you lack a core from which to guide your actions. As a result,

any actions you take will likely be haphazard, and dictated by thoughts and emotions rather than a definite sense of what is important to you. These actions take you further away from who and where you want to be.

Small strategies that lead to psychological flexibility

The Power of Small is all about learning how to move towards psychological flexibility. The strategies fall under three headings:

1. **Awareness of the present moment**
   You can learn how to reconnect with the present moment, through which you will become a more flexible, wise and compassionate thinker.

2. **Openness to unwanted experiences**
   You can learn how to break out of thinking and emotional traps and instead observe your thoughts and emotions in helpful and effective ways.

3. **Engagement with what matters**
   You can learn how to connect to what truly matters to you and what you want your life to be about, allowing these core values to guide a sequence of small actions that build up over time to radically change the course of your life.

The Power of Small will teach you all of these strategies, so that you can become far more psychologically flexible in your life. You will still think unwanted thoughts and feel unwanted feelings (you're only human, after all), but the extent to which these throw you off course will greatly diminish.

As you work through this book, you will acquire an ever-growing toolkit of small skills that we will teach you, one manageable step at a time. This psychologically flexible toolkit will help you to respond from your core values in even the most distressing of situations.

TODAY'S SMALL STEP

Assess your psychological flexibility

Here are three questions to help you gauge where you are on the psychological flexibility spectrum. From zero to nine, indicate how often you get caught up in these activities, which result in your becoming more psychologically inflexible.

Zero indicates never. Nine indicates all the time. Five represents about half the time.

1. Are you completely lost in your thoughts about things that have happened, or things that might happen? Things you have done, or things you have to, or want to do?

2. Do you get so blinkered by your thoughts and feelings that they become overwhelming?

3. Do you run around from one thing to the next,
    always doing something but not really getting
    anywhere? On the other end of the spectrum, yet
    equally problematic, do you always think about
    doing something different and meaningful but
    never quite get around to doing it?

Your score gives you an idea of where you are right now
– and what you can work towards. The Power of Small will
show you how to increase your psychological flexibility, in
ways that will create space for movement and change of
whatever unhelpful thought patterns and behaviour habits
dominate for you.

Part One

The Comfort Trap

1
The Comfort Zone

It is impossible to live without failing at something, unless you live so cautiously that you might as well not have lived at all – in which case, you fail by default. JK Rowling

Feeling overwhelmed looks very different for each of us. How it impacts us depends very much on what we have going on in life, and also on our earlier life experiences. For example, if we have had a lot of trauma in our life, this may greatly affect how we respond to our sense of overwhelm. Interestingly, some people with a history of traumatic events see themselves as great in a crisis. They go into 'do-do go-go' mode, doing pretty much anything other than actually stopping and acknowledging how they are feeling. Other people go into complete lockdown, when it seems like absolutely nothing is possible, from brushing your teeth and feeding yourself nutritiously, to texting and calling family and friends.

Generally, though, we tend to get tipped into overwhelm when we face problems that seem too powerful, or beyond our capacity to deal with, or when we experience an intense emotion we don't think we can manage.

It's important to acknowledge that unwanted emotions, such as stress, can have extremely positive influences on our lives. We absolutely need to encounter situations and tasks that at least appear outside of our comfort zone. This is where growth happens. Without stress, we would live very boring and uneventful lives.

Staying comfortable is remaining static. If you don't break out of what you usually do, you stave off the possibility for meaningful change in your life. But the problem is that when we move too far outside our comfort zone, we end up with an unworkable sense of overwhelm. For manageable change, we need to learn to gently push the boundaries of our comfort zone, using the Small approach this book will teach you, in incremental, gradual, safe steps.

We are, by nature, all or nothing creatures. Most of us have a tendency to either procrastinate our lives away, or run life at a speed that is unmanageable and unsustainable in the long term. Chances are you know a lot about all or nothing. You most likely know a lot about either setting your standards and goals too high; or buying into the story that you are not able for very much at all. Many of us flit from one end of this spectrum to the other.

As we embark on this journey together, we invite you to gently break out of your comfort zone, by engaging with this book in a connected way that offers you a new experience. For those of us who go at things all guns blazing at the start and then fall off the wagon, a note of caution: the Small way means the gradual expansion of our comfort zone, little by little, so that the sources of your overwhelm diminish as you acquire the skills you need to bring your life into balance and harmony.

So, before we go any further, we'd like to invite you to connect to your underlying intention for reading this book. Is it because you're overwhelmed by the stresses of daily life – the overflowing inbox, the never-ending to-do list, the apparently impossible task of keeping everyone happy while eating a balanced diet, getting eight hours' sleep a night, and your 30 minutes of exercise every day, still looking like you're perfectly fine?

Or perhaps you're at a stage in life where a significant person is no longer with you, whether through death, the breakdown of a relationship, or someone moving away. Maybe you are in a job you dislike and you feel more and more stuck, or maybe you have too much responsibility and more is being piled on you every day. Maybe you are in financial difficulty and don't know how to find a way out. Whatever is overwhelming you, this book is about using small and simple steps to move forward.

It is extremely tempting to want to change all areas of your life all at once. However, we have found time and again that you will make the most significant impact if you start with one valued area. This is not to say that you will only ever focus on this one area through the Power of Small. Quite the opposite, in fact. However, it is best to start with that part of your life where you believe the most positive impact can be achieved, right this moment.

TODAY'S SMALL STEP

Identify your comfort zone

In your small steps diary, write down three actions you take to keep yourself in your comfort zone. They could be things like drinking wine every evening, staying in rather than going out, or avoiding a particular task that you know needs to be done yet you can't seem to get around to. Only you will know what you do to keep yourself in a safe, unchallenged place. This is a chance to give yourself space to think about what those actions are, and assess whether or not they are helpful. And if you're feeling courageous and want to maximise what you get out of this book, also identify at least one cost for each of your comfort zone actions.

It is through this process of identification that change begins.

2
The Self-Care Zone

Self-care is never a selfish act – it is simply good stewardship of the only gift I have, the gift I was put on earth to offer to others.
Parker Palmer

Just as no positive growth can be experienced without venturing outside of the comfort zone, it is also true that if we move too far outside it too quickly, we can also move outside our self-care zone, thereby losing the potential for sustainable change. If we stay within our self-care zone, however, we can transform our lives in incredibly positive ways. We start to respond differently in relationships. We find ourselves capable of more than we ever knew possible.

When our sense of being overwhelmed is such that we are unable to do anything to change it, our task is not to completely eradicate it but to find a way to transform it into something manageable.

Left unchecked, overwhelm can lead to us acting in ways that erode our health and wellbeing, our relationships with ourselves and others, and our sense of fun and general positive engagement with life.

Generally, overwhelm is something that builds up over time. The daily triggers, such as stress, are often manageable, but when a more significant stress gets added into the mix, things can tip over, and what was manageable before no longer is. Some examples of tipping points are a big move, losing someone dear to us, or having a baby. If we are already stretched, these experiences have the potential to really blindside us, and if we have already been repeatedly stressed over a long period of time, we can find ourselves very low and vulnerable.

Take a look at the Power of Small TEDx talk to see a visual representation of the self-care zone.

Breaking away too far

When seeking change, many people run into trouble by trying to break too far outside of their comfort zone, so that they are also outside of their self-care zone. For example, if you have trouble asserting your needs, it will most likely be outside of your self-care zone to start telling everyone every time they bother you. If it's in your comfort zone to devote your time and energy to other people, it will most likely be outside your self-care zone to block off large chunks of time in your diary to look after your own needs.

If asserting your needs is a problem for you, your

comfort zone often involves a whole lot of small actions around pushing down your feelings and needs and putting others before you. You most likely find it harder to honour commitments to yourself than to others. One way to break outside of your comfort zone, yet remain firmly planted within your self-care zone, is to choose one person to assert your needs to first. In order to remain within your self-care zone, it is best to choose someone who is particularly empathic and understanding.

If you are on the opposite end of the spectrum and are prone to flying off the handle, or reacting to circumstances and opinions in a way that leads you into difficult situations, then it would be impossible to expect you to make the big leap to consistently giving feedback in measured and compassionate ways. However, one step outside of your comfort zone, yet still firmly planted within your self-care zone, would be to sit down and quickly write out whatever is bothering you on a piece of paper. Rather than sending this as an email or text message to the offending party, however, wait ten minutes before looking back over what you've written. This will help create some distance between your thoughts and your reactions. As you get more comfortable with waiting ten minutes, you could gradually increase the amount of time before telling people how you're feeling.

The small step you need to take very much depends on what your comfort zone is right now; it's about breaking out just a little from your default ways of reacting.

The self-care zone involves two critical components: a)

taking small enough steps that are manageable for you in the long term, and b) building moments into your day that nurture and nourish you. Every action we engage in or avoid has an impact. Some actions nurture and nourish us and some deplete us. What nurtures and nourishes you is going to depend on your personality and how introverted or extroverted you are.

We all need a certain amount of nurturing activities that involve others, such as meeting friends or engaging in interactive hobbies. However, we equally need some nurturing activities in our lives that bring us a sense of peace and solitude. Therefore, it's of critical importance that you balance both introverted and extroverted self-care activities.

5-minute Breakouts

One of the core tools of the Power of Small is the 5-minute breakout. Put simply, it involves taking five minutes to do something that is outside of your comfort zone, yet firmly planted within your self-care zone. For some of us, this 5-minute breakout will involve slowing down and taking things off our plate, whilst for others, it may involve deliberately taking conscious steps towards facing a challenge that we have been avoiding.

Being overwhelmed is often a kind of circle with no end. Because we're overwhelmed, we feel unable to do anything about what's overwhelming us, and because we can't do anything, we remain overwhelmed. The 5-minute breakout is about breaking that circle for just five minutes in a gentle way, taking a tiny amount of time to help change this self-perpetuating story. It may involve doing something that is initially uncomfortable, or something that is comforting, something that is action driven, or something that is about stopping all activity; one way or the other, as our practice with clients has shown time and time again, the 5-minute breakout is an invaluable tool for a life less overwhelmed in the long term.

Some examples of 5-minute breakouts

Sean is overwhelmed by unpaid bills. Instead of opening new bills that arrive, he leaves them in a pile with the other bills that he hasn't felt able to face. It's a growing pile, and as it grows, Sean becomes more and more overwhelmed.

A possible 5-minute breakout for Sean would be to consciously connect to the cost of avoiding these bills, such as the growing interest and late fees as each week passes, and the regular arguments with his partner about the financial stress impacting their relationship. He could then openly and honestly recognise how his avoidant actions are moving him away from what really matters to him. He could then find space to reconnect with what is truly important to him; a more loving and harmonious relationship and taking care of his responsibilities.

Rather than getting caught up in his usual overwhelming cycle of letting the bills build up over months and then tackling them all at once, Sean could use a 5 minute breakout. He could take only one bill, sit at a table, breathe deeply in and out four or five times, and then open it. He could read the amount on the bill and notice any uncomfortable emotions or unwanted thoughts arising.

Sean could choose to close his eyes, reconnect with the pain of avoiding paying this bill and consciously choose to clear just that one debt from his life. If it is within Sean's self-care zone, he can continue this process for up to five minutes, looking at approximately three bills in this conscious deliberate way.

The 5-minute breakout is less about thinking or feeling about the situation in a different way, at least in the immediate term, and more about *responding* in a different way. This different way of responding might very well be temporarily uncomfortable; yet ultimately it is more helpful, and makes our life a lot more manageable and less overwhelming in the long term.

Emily is overwhelmed by the demands that her frail and elderly mother puts on her every day. Emily has her own family and work to attend to, but her mother doesn't seem to understand and expects her to be at her beck and call. Emily initially couldn't bear to refuse her mother because she loves her dearly, and the guilt felt like it would be too much.

A possible 5-minute breakout for Emily would be to connect to, not only what kind of daughter she would like to be, but also what kind of person she would like to be across all aspects of her life. If Emily didn't have other roles in her life, not limited to being a mother, team leader and friend, perhaps it would be workable for her to say yes to every request her mother makes. However, the reality is that Emily has another number of roles outside being a daughter, and there is a direct impact on each of these roles when she spreads herself too thin.

Once Emily has connected to the values underlying the various different areas of her life, she then needs to take an overall view of what is manageable and realistic for her to do for her mother. She can then make a values-guided priority list.

With some practical thought, Emily can identify what the priorities are and then commit to those and nothing else, just for the moment. Emily could then pinpoint that the most essential elements to her mother's care were ensuring her mother had some nutritious food daily, a weekly shop, and a visit every second day where they left the house.

When her mother makes her next demand, Emily could take a 30-second breakout to internally check if this demand is part of the priority list for her mother's care. If it's not, she could tell her mother she can't do that today. It's important to note that Emily may very well still feel guilty when she says no to her mother. This is part of her learning and life history. However, providing Emily has taken her breakout to connect to what matters and consciously chooses her actions, she can rest in knowing that she is making the most effective choice grounded in her values, even if it brings some discomfort in the moment.

Alex is overwhelmed at the thought of giving a presentation at work. She grows more anxious as the presentation date gets closer, and yet she keeps putting off her preparation. Every time she thinks about sitting down to prepare, her heart starts racing and she feels nauseous. She also knows that not doing anything has her in panic mode, so it's double the overwhelm.

A possible 5-minute breakout for Alex would be to connect to her reason underlying doing this presentation in the first place. More than being part of her job description, the primary reason is because she truly believes in the project she has been working hard on. She wants to share with her team how the project will help the company and its employees. When Alex allows some space, she can also recognise that public speaking in general would allow her more freedom to communicate what she believed in to others.

Alex was encouraged by connecting to the meaning underlying her presentation, but that didn't take away how anxious she felt. She also noticed that she is very afraid of unfavourable feedback from others, and when she becomes blinkered by this, she avoids preparing, as it leads to her confronting these fears head on.

Alex could then put a brief plan in place whereby she will jot down the main points tomorrow for five minutes, explore some examples the day after, and so on. She is still afraid of the presentation and continues to be concerned about others' opinions of her; however, the presentation now feels more manageable and more meaningful. In taking these small steps over a five minute period, Alex will have broken the circle of overwhelm and simply begun the work she needs to do.

Throughout this book, we'll be giving you examples of 5-minute breakouts various people have used in their daily lives, which gave them foundational help in tackling the situations that were overwhelming them. Once you get a better sense of how others have practically used these small steps to help make important changes, you'll be easily able to come up with your own 5-minute breakouts. You will then have a simple, yet powerful tool, that you can call upon in even the most overwhelming of situations.

It is our philosophy that the answer to the modern condition of being overwhelmed is not only better management of all that's on your plate, but also slowly simplifying what's on it to begin with. Constructive life change does not come instantly, as when the answers you've been waiting for arrive like a bolt of lightning from the sky and suddenly it all makes sense.

The Power of Small says that for today, if the only change you can make to begin to address the problem of feeling overwhelmed is to take a five minute walk outside your house, or to create two minutes in your busy day to simply sit still and connect with your breathing, then that is a powerful, dynamic act worth doing. And from that small acorn, much growth can happen.

TODAY'S SMALL STEP

Identify your self-care actions

Take out your small steps diary, draw a circle next to your comfort zone, and label this your self-care zone. In this

self-care zone, write down a number of actions that would
bring you outside your comfort zone, yet feel small and
manageable enough that they would be within your self-
care zone to do. These are your 5-minute breakout actions.
Now commit to engaging in one of these actions, for just five
minutes. Similarly to the situations we shared with you here,
we recommend that you connect to the values underlying
each 5-minute breakout first, as this will help to motivate
you into action.

3

The Life Worth
Fighting For Zone

*The secret to achieving inner peace lies in understanding our inner
core values – those things in our lives that are most important to
us – and then seeing that they are reflected in the daily events
of our lives.* Hyrum W Smith

Our values connect us with what matters in our lives.
Grounding ourselves regularly in our values is vitally
important as we take the journey of change that comes with
this book. Our values should always be our guides. Change
that does not connect with our values will inevitably be
short-lived, unfulfilling, or both.

Throughout this book, you will be asked to look at aspects
of your internal world – in the form of thoughts, emotions,
bodily sensations and memories – and your external world –
in terms of your actions and your relationships with others.
Often the experience of looking at these parts of your life

can be unfamiliar and painful. If it wasn't, chances are you'd be looking at and addressing these aspects already, and you possibly wouldn't need this book. Looking at these internal and external parts of our life in a systematic and gradual way brings us closer and closer to living the majority of our life within the Life Worth Fighting For Zone.

What are values?

What do we mean when we talk about values? Values transcend the logical and rational processing areas of our brain. Like the air we breathe, our values are always present and around us, whether we are aware of them or not.

When we talk about our values we identify what is meaningful and purposeful in our lives. It is helpful to ask ourselves deep within our hearts: what truly matters to me?

Values essentially are the small blocks that, when tuned into, build up over time to create the life that you truly want and desire. When we are either disconnected from or not living in line with our values, these small blocks build up over time to create a life that is unfulfilling, and lacking a sense of purpose and direction.

Values involve looking deep inside your heart to see what is most important to you. If you simply ask yourself, 'What are my values?', you'll often just list off things you *think* you should be, such as kind, loyal, caring, successful, and so on. There is nothing wrong with any of these characteristics per se, but the mark of truly identifying our values is authenticity – when you know deep down, in your bones, that this is the case.

Alternatively, you may be someone who finds it difficult to identify your core values – and this often indicates a person who spends much of their time trying to outrun their fears. More of this anon.

In order for values to be values, they need to be freely chosen and in line with some internal barometer, rather than obligations or expectations placed on us by others. Sometimes, our values might be very similar to those of our family and friends, and sometimes they might be radically different. However, values will feel lighter and more empowering when they are freely chosen rather than subconsciously and automatically inherited from others.

It can be more helpful to ask yourself some practical questions about valued areas of your life, such as relationships, health and personal growth, purpose and contribution, and recreation.

Clarifying our values

With the Power of Small, you start to identify your values first in broad terms so that each small goal you set in your life brings you one step closer to who and where you want to be. In this way, when you act you are guided by your life purpose and values. Here are five questions that are aimed at helping you establish your inner core values.

1. How do you want to be remembered by others?

2. What words would you like your loved ones to use when describing you?

3. What were your childhood dreams?

4. What are the three qualities that are most important to you? For example, kindness, open-mindedness, compassion.

5. What brings you the most joy in the world?

What values are not

Sometimes, to really identify what something is, it can be helpful to look at what it is not. Let's walk you through some of the common misconceptions that can become stumbling blocks to lasting and fulfilling change.

Values are not rigid rules that are insensitive to context about what you should and should not do. The belief that values are such rigid rules leads to many of us struggling greatly. Values are not shoulds or musts.

We can set excessively high and rigid expectations for ourselves and others, which can be a breeding ground for disappointment, anxiety, depression and a general dissatisfaction and stagnancy in life. A seemingly innocent example of this is valuing kindness and then believing that you, or others, need to be kind in all contexts, irrespective of how other people treat you.

Values are not dependent on an outcome or results, which can be hard for us to understand in this increasingly achievement-driven world.

There is a danger that we obediently live out our days,

steering our life course in the direction of predetermined goals or milestones, often based on expectations and judgements – usually other people's. What we encourage you to do is to take life as it comes and meet it on your own terms and in accordance with your own values – those things that matter most to you.

This is the key difference between being nudged mindlessly through your day by expectations and rules, and living your life through conscious and freely chosen actions.

Values are not what you want or need from others – because what others give you falls outside your control. Values come from within.

Values reflected in our daily lives

It is not enough simply to know what your values are. In fact, you can encounter a great deal of pain and suffering if you know what your inner core values are when the everyday small actions you engage in are not in line with these values. Knowing your values is the first important step. The second step is learning to act in accordance with these values.

Values don't exist in one time or place, nor are they like goals set for the future that once you achieve them, you'll have ticked off your list for good. Values are more of a regular diet than a medicine or fix. Just like eating dinner won't prevent you from feeling hunger again, living according to your values in one situation won't transform you or cure you. That's why you need to consciously connect every day with how you want your values to play out in your life.

The Power of Small way of living is all about repeatedly checking in with your taken-for-granted assumptions. This prompts you to look a little deeper to make sure you are continually engaging with who and where you want to be. Which can change. Therefore, you need multiple small moments to establish and re-establish your values, rather than spending considerable time on a one-off situation and following the values that stem from it blindly, even when your life and life circumstances change.

Over time, this checking-in process will build to create your life worth fighting for.

TODAY'S SMALL STEP

Establish your core values

In your small steps diary write your answer to one of the five values clarification questions outlined in this chapter. Here is a gentle reminder of the questions:

Values clarification questions:

1. How do you want to be remembered by others?

2. What words would you like your loved ones to use when describing you?

3. What were your childhood dreams?

4. What are the three qualities that are most
    important to you? For example, kindness, open-
    mindedness, compassion.

5. What brings you the most joy in the world?

Maybe pick one that feels a bit outside your comfort zone, but stay within your self-care zone when answering it by being as honest and gentle with yourself as possible. If that goes well, try answering another of the questions. Then look at the words you've written. What are the key adjectives? Write them down individually. They are your core values.

Remember that knowing your values is the first important step. When you're ready, turn the page so that you can start to see these values reflected in the daily events of your life.

4
Small Actions, Big Impact

The truth that many people never understand, until it is too late, is that the more you try to avoid suffering the more you suffer because smaller and more insignificant things begin to torture you in proportion to your fear of being hurt. Thomas Merton

Every small action or inaction we encounter on a daily basis has an impact on how we live. In any given situation there is usually the chance to take action that will bring us closer to who and where we want to be in a particular valued area of our lives. There is also at least one action that we could take that will bring us further away from who we want to be and where we want to go.

Small stressors, big impact

In the modern-day world, we act like it's only the big stuff that counts – the births, deaths, marriages, divorces, new jobs, job transitions and home moves. However, research has indicated that, although they may seem trivial or manageable in themselves, small everyday stressors can have just as much impact on our lives if they are left to build up over time – the overflowing inboxes, the person who was rude to you in the shop, the traffic that wakes you up every morning, the construction work that has been going on for months now, the unoccupied home with the faulty alarm that keeps going off at stupid o'clock….

Each and every one of these events has an impact on our psychological health. How we respond to such seemingly small stressors has a huge impact on how satisfied or dissatisfied we are with the course of our lives.

How you choose to respond to every small interaction that you have with yourself and others on a daily basis has the power to influence the direction you take next. Do you tend to scold yourself for feeling sad or anxious about something 'silly', or choose to respond to your emotions with kindness and compassion? Do you push down your own needs in order to be what you think others want you to be, or take the risk of falling out of favour with others by communicating your needs in an authentic way? Do you turn to chocolate, alcohol, or other stimulants, such as the internet, when the going gets tough, or do you take a moment to pause, and contemplate your response to a challenging situation before you jump to fix it? How we respond to daily events and interactions impacts deeply on the quality of our lives.

It's easy to go about life pretending that all these little actions don't count. But they do. And there's only so long you can get away with just putting up with all of these daily stressors, pushing them down or running away from them before they catch up with you in a very big way.

So many people go through life in a perpetual cycle of running themselves down into the ground without taking the small moments to take care of themselves. We are constantly expecting our bodies and minds to perform at an optimal level. Meanwhile, the vast majority of us have a range of small, persistent habits that lead to big problems.

For some of you, this will be around the way you physically take care of yourselves – you under or oversleep, you eat far too much processed food, and you don't exercise enough. Or you overdrink, or you subscribe to the work hard, play hard motto, which has you on a perpetual loop of feeling like you just need to catch a breath.

Others of you will have persistent, problematic habits around not taking care of your psychological health and wellbeing. You give yourself an incredibly hard time for every small thing you do that doesn't match up to your high standards. You frequently go into shame mode, where you demonise yourself and devalue your worth as a human being, based on some feeling you have or some action you engaged in. You know the skills you need to learn to help you with your sense of overwhelm or anxiety, yet you frequently let your own psychological wellbeing move to the bottom of the list. You allow your internal world to dictate what you do and don't do in the external world, in ways that take you away from who you want to be.

It is important to realise that every small action has an impact. However, it is equally important to treat ourselves gently. As Pema Chödrön, the North American Buddhist nun and author of several books, including *Start Where You Are,* says: 'We need to treat ourselves with both honesty and gentleness.'

Toward and away moves

With the Power of Small approach, we deliberately do not label our actions as good or bad, right or wrong. Such judgemental tags frequently put us into a shame cycle where we end up repeating the same old ineffective patterns that made us – and keep us – overwhelmed in the first place. Using what we call toward and away moves is a far more self-caring and effective way of changing our actions in small ways.

Imagine you are trying to get to a place you've never been to before and you end up lost. The moment you realise you're moving further away from where you want to be, you redirect yourself as quickly as possible and start moving closer towards your desired destination. However, we often do the exact opposite of this in the psychological world.

For instance, let's say you're trying to eat more healthily. Many of you will start saying that you are 'good' when you're eating things that are healthy for you, and label yourself as 'bad' when you eat unhealthy foods. However, when you get into this cycle of labelling yourself as bad, the initial small action of eating one unhealthy item of food can soon evolve into a shame cycle where you continue to eat unhealthily.

If you were using toward and away moves, you would very quickly be able to pinpoint the action you need to take to bring you back towards your values and goals, instead of moving further away from them.

Toward moves include any action you engage in that will help you move closer to your values. Toward moves can often involve some short-term discomfort, yet invariably bring you closer to long term fulfilment.

Away moves include any action you engage in that brings you away from a given value, with the intention of avoiding an uncomfortable experience; for example, eating that large bag of crisps which you know is not an act of self-care, but that provides a short-term release from an unwanted emotion such as anxiety. Away moves could also involve engaging in a particular action or inaction in an attempt to avoid potential rejection or failure.

Michelle: toward and away moves in action

When Michelle came for support she was overweight and engaged in lots of away moves around food. Michelle wanted to improve her physical health and psychological wellbeing through eating more healthy, nutritious foods and less processed foods. Her relationship with food also negatively impacted her psychological wellbeing, as she felt so bad about her weight that she avoided family and friends.

Michelle's away moves (which ended up being massive away moves because she did them so frequently) included eating multipacks of jellies every week; keeping sweets, chocolate and crisps in her car; and having takeaway three times a week.

Michelle had tried numerous diets. She generally started off all guns blazing and lost a lot of weight in the first couple of weeks. However, she could never stick to these restrictive eating regimes, and each time she went on a diet or joined a slimming club, she would ultimately put on more weight in the long term than she had lost to begin with.

Michelle was more than a little fed up with the process. She found it hard to believe that she could ever make big changes in this area of her life. We worked with Michelle in a totally different way than she'd been used to previously. Rather than make a lot of changes all at once, we drew up a list of her away moves and together started changing them, one at a time. For example, one of the first changes she made was to stop buying multipacks. The deal was that she could eat as much chocolate as she liked, but could only buy one item of chocolate or sweets on any given shopping trip. This one small change alone led to Michelle losing ten pounds in the first three weeks. We then gradually decreased the number of takeaways per week in favour of healthier alternatives.

Whenever Michelle recognised that she was engaging in an away move around food, she took a breath, offered herself the same kindness she would offer someone she cared about, and made an active choice to engage in one small toward move.

A toward move is any action that helped Michelle move

toward her goal of physical health and wellbeing. This involved stopping eating any further unhealthy foods when previously she might have thought, 'I might as well be hung for a sheep as a lamb', or 'I'll get back on track on Monday'.

The Power of Small is about making a minor change now rather than the often unfulfilled promise of a major change later.

Michelle's 5-minute breakout

The key 5-minute breakout that helped Michelle was what she called 'choice time'. Whenever she was tempted to order a takeaway, or maybe buy a six-pack of crisps in the supermarket, Michelle began taking a mental breakout to consider the idea that she had a choice, and what the likely consequences were of both choices. She closed her eyes and allowed herself to consider what would happen if she bought the takeaway or multipack. While it might feel relieving in the short term, in the long term it would most likely bring pain and discomfort in terms of gaining weight and reduced self-confidence. Michelle also considered what would most likely happen if she chose not to but the multipack or takeaway. She noticed and acknowledged the painful emotions that would likely arise in the short-term, such as anxiety, sadness or boredom, and also what the long term consequences would be of a healthier lifestyle and increased sense of self-acceptance.

At the beginning, Michelle often made the choice to get the takeaway she craved, but by repeatedly taking five minutes to break the circle of overwhelm with 'choice time', she ultimately began making more and more toward moves for her long-term physical health and wellbeing.

TODAY'S SMALL STEP

What small actions have the biggest impact on your life?

In your small steps diary write down one aspect of your life that you would like to change. Now identify and write down three small away moves that bring you further away from who and where you want to be in this regard.

Then identify three small toward moves that can bring you closer to who and where you want to be.

Be careful not to choose toward moves that are too big, as this will lead to a sense of overwhelm. For example, with Michelle it would have been too large a jump to move from eating large quantities of chocolate and sweets to not eating them at all. Pick toward moves that might be significant enough to have an impact on your life, yet small enough to be manageable and sustainable on an ongoing basis.

Take a look at your three toward moves. For each, ask yourself honestly and gently how confident you are that you will follow through on this move instead of one of your away moves. If you are at least 80 per cent confident, you are on track; if less than that, there is a chance that this toward move is too big for now, so see if you can find one that is a bit smaller and feels more manageable. You can always work your way up to the toward move that you originally chose.

We all engage in both toward and away moves for very good reasons, which we will address in the next chapter. Honesty and gentleness are key here. This is the mode by which you are most likely to make the most meaningful small changes in your daily life that lead to massive changes in your overall quality of life.

5

The Bigger, Better, Faster Conflict

The reason we struggle with insecurity is because we compare our behind-the-scenes with everyone else's highlight reel.
Steven Furtick

Humans are complex creatures. We seek change, but at the same time are absolutely petrified by it. We wish to be spontaneous, yet also crave routine, structure and predictability. Forming the basis of these conflicts is another, much deeper, internal struggle, which goes back to our very foundations.

Despite the evolution of the human race, we are all hardwired by our hunter-gatherer beginnings. From generation to generation, since the dawn of time, we have remained primarily motivated by a desire to survive.

Our prehistoric ancestors who were isolated or who got into unpredictable situations with little regard for their safety, generally didn't stay alive for too long. Those who were members of the biggest social circles, who were strong and brave enough to keep themselves fed, while being clever enough not to end up as someone else's lunch, survived.

We're still the same survivors on a fundamental level, but another way of being has evolved over time – we grew to want to thrive in the world rather than simply survive. And to this end we often strive for ideals of success, with actions intended towards being bigger, better and faster.

This striving can lead us towards two modes of coping with day-to-day life: do-do, go-go and back away, not today. They are two ultimately unmanageable sides of the same coin, both aimed at increasing our chances of comfort and decreasing the likelihood of experiencing discomfort. Whenever we are overextending ourselves in one area of our lives, we are inevitably underextending ourselves in another area. Therefore, the vast majority of us will go into do-do, go-go mode in some areas while simultaneously engaging in back away, not today mode in another.

Do-do, go-go

If you commit to giving more time than you have to spend, you will constantly be running from time debt collectors. Elizabeth Grace Saunders

When we are in do-do, go-go mode, we relentlessly drive our actions, often to the point of burnout, towards ever-increasing, unrealistic ideals. We have overly packed schedules and are constantly on the move. We continuously stretch ourselves beyond our physical and mental limits until forced to stop. Then, inevitably, when we do not match up to our unrealistic expectations, we judge ourselves harshly.

Back away, not today

What is not started today is never finished tomorrow.
Johann Wolfgang von Goethe

When we are in back away, not today mode, we avoid the pressure of trying to realise our own too-high expectations. We become completely paralysed as our must-do list continues to stack up. We back away from others and keep putting off difficult tasks, in a never-ending cycle of despair.

Important note

These two ways of being are not mutually exclusive. We have worked with many people who are in do-do, go-go mode at work – where they appear super confident and often overextend themselves to burnout – and back away, not today mode in relationships – where they avoid voicing their feelings for fear of conflict with members of their own family or their partner. The vast majority of us will engage in do-do, go-go in some areas and back away, not today in others.

For example, let's take a look at two friends, Alex and Jamie. Alex goes into do-do, go-go mode at work. She often works 60-plus hours a week and she'll attend many additional meetings in that time. Simultaneously, she is in firm back away, not today mode around relationships since she broke up with her ex-girlfriend two years ago. Alex was heartbroken after this break-up. She has poured herself even more into work than before, while firmly avoiding any possibility of meeting a new partner.

On the other hand, Jamie is in back away, not today mode in her work life. She is in a job with minimal responsibility, and minimal job satisfaction to go with it. Jamie often complains to Alex and her other friends about how frustrating her job is, yet she doesn't apply for new jobs or attend courses that could advance her career prospects. In her social life, Jamie is in do-do, go-go mode; she tends to have plans five or six nights a week, which often involve drinking alcohol. Whenever a relationship ends for Jamie, she goes straight onto online dating with the motto, there's plenty more fish in the sea.

Depending on what we are trying to avoid, it is very common to go all out in one area of our life, while long-arming another area completely.

Is bigger better?

Beyond the evolutionary hardwiring that we all share, there are many cultural messages that feed our pursuit to be bigger, better, faster. Switch on your radio or television, or open up your social media account and you'll be bombarded by messages telling you why you must strive for more. A strong cultural narrative builds, which gives us the impression that unless we are special – and by special we mean better than others – then we are somehow flawed or inferior. These lessons about having to be special, having to be the best, having to own better things and so forth, are so ubiquitous that most of us learn them as young children. On a deep level, they are the seeds for the self-defeating belief that we can never be good enough.

If this belief is left unquestioned, we will spend the rest of our lives either trying to hide those parts of us that we fear will be rejected by others, or desperately striving to be bigger and better. Both states lead to overwhelm.

David's back away, not today story

David started learning about the Power of Small approach because he desperately wanted to be in a loving relationship, but since he struggled with severe social anxiety, he was unable to form lasting attachments to the opposite sex. Recently he'd gone on a few dates via a dating app, and while he could hold a conversation over text messages, when he met a woman in person he found himself unable to properly function. He could barely talk or even make eye contact, and his dates slowly ground to an awkward halt. Increasingly he realised that the women he met didn't want to see him again.

David did what many people in a very difficult situation do – he went into back away, not today mode. When he had an unwanted experience he would take himself off dating apps for a couple of months. He would also become quite reclusive, avoiding social occasions, particularly ones involving people he didn't know.

This avoidance of anxiety in an attempt to make himself more comfortable actually made him *less* comfortable. David's comfort zone got smaller and smaller, and eventually he felt paralysed.

David's 5-minute breakout

David used a variety of 5-minute breakouts to help his social anxiety in dating situations. He started by doing visualisations where he would imagine engaging with others. We also role played conversations with 'new' people. Our objective was to begin by helping David gently push the boundaries of the claustrophobic comfort zone he'd become trapped in. At the same time, we firmly connected to the motivation that was big enough to encourage him to break free from his comfort zone — his desire to be in a loving relationship.

Then we began to delve into David's away moves and toward moves, in terms of dating.

David's away moves were getting caught up in his head on the real date, shutting down communication and giving himself a hard time for having anxiety.

His toward moves were to connect to his date via the app and be able to hold a conversation by text, asking her questions about herself, being genuinely interested and able to reply, talking about himself too.

We identified three toward moves David could use when he went on dates. He could use a skill he was adept at when engaging in text conversations on the dating app, which he identified as 'being polite and being humorous'. He could use his skill for asking questions and being interested. And he could use his skill for sharing information about himself.

With his away moves also clearly marked out, David took the small step of going back online and looking at profiles of people he might be interested in seeing. Soon he had connected with a woman, and instead of jumping too far out of his comfort zone by asking her to dinner, he asked her to have coffee with him on an afternoon, a toward move that was within his self-care zone.

We prepared David for his coffee date by prompting him to engage in one of his toward moves when he noticed he was getting caught up in an away move. So, for instance, if he felt he was getting caught up in his head, he could break the cycle by asking his date a question about herself, or telling her something about himself. He could tell her that he often got nervous on dates, breaking the ice on his social anxiety.

Wanting to thrive in the world rather than simply survive, David had been trying to find a partner, which of course is a perfectly natural thing. However, he became fixated with certain characteristics that he imagined would be desirable to a potential partner, and he viewed his social anxiety as not being one of those things. In his quest to hide this aspect of himself, which he believed to be unlovable, he in fact decreased his chances of finding and connecting to a partner.

However, through learning that unwanted emotions and discomfort are part of the price of admission to intimacy, and learning small skills to change his relationship with this discomfort, his life started to open up again. We'll come back to this in more detail later.

TODAY'S SMALL STEP

What do your do-do, go-go and back away, not today modes look like?

Open your small steps diary on a fresh set of pages. Draw two boxes on each page. Across the top of the left page, write 'Do-Do, Go-Go' and write 'Back Away, Not Today' on the top of the right page. In the left-handside box on the left page, write three actions you engage in when you are in do-do, go-go mode. Do the same in the left-hand side box on the right page, this time in relation to back away, not today actions that you take in your daily life. See the figure below for a clear illustration of how this will look in your small steps diary.

In the right-hand-side box on each page, write three unwanted effects this can have on you.

Examples:

Do-Do, Go-Go		Back Away, Not Today	
Actions	Unwanted Consequences	Actions	Unwanted Consequences
Overpack my week	I am almost always running late	I don't say no to people	I end up feeling resentful
Don't allow enough time to go from one activity to the next	I feel exhausted and like I can never catch up on myself	I don't plan ahead and make healthy food for myself	I've put on 15 lbs over the past year
Say yes too much	I neglect my own health and wellbeing	I keep joining gyms but rarely actually go	I notice I'm getting breathless when I walk up stairs

Small change: I will make a list tomorrow morning of the things I have to do for the day, and prioritise them under the headings 'Important' and 'Not So Important'. I will concentrate on getting the important things done only.

6
Short-Term Pain, Long-Term Gain

The whole of life is, after all, a process of walking on a tightrope.
If you do not fall one way you fall the other, and each is
equally bad. Aldous Huxley

Every single day we go through countless experiences that offer us the opportunity to either move towards what matters to us most, or in the opposite direction. Usually we make lots of little decisions that steer us further away by trying to avoid something unwanted. For instance, a neighbour asks you to help him by dropping him to the airport, which would usually be fine, except you're on a tight deadline. The tight deadline matters to you most, but still you say yes because you don't want to upset your neighbour, plus you're worried that if you don't help him out, he'll say no to you next time you ask him for a favour.

Although we might not even realise it at the time, often these small and seemingly insignificant choices we make are either the building blocks of a rich and meaningful life, or the stumbling blocks that stop us from getting there. There is power in each of the small moves you make as you negotiate the dilemmas you are presented with throughout your day. Many of our away moves are not explicitly motivated by a desire to move away from what's important to us but instead, more often than not, by a desire to minimise or avoid some unwanted discomfort. However, those away moves very often have the unintended side effect of also bringing us further away from who and where we want to be.

This book is about building a skill set so that you can connect with what's important to you when these little dilemmas occur, and as a result, make toward moves instead of away moves. With small steps, you will start to take more and more toward moves in more situations, with more and more people. For now, though, let's explore the types of toward and away moves people tend to have difficulty with.

Identifying toward and away moves

Toward and away moves are as individual as we are. It all depends on how you intend for these behaviours to function in relation to your values.

For example, Jill and Rachel both engage in the same action of interrupting a discussion going on in this week's team meeting. For Jill this is a big toward move. She's been connected to the conversation, noticed an important contribution she could make and, despite feeling really anxious about speaking out, she presents her ideas because she believes they will be helpful to the project in the long run.

On the other hand, this same action is an away move on this occasion for Rachel. She's been zoned out for most of the meeting, worrying about her boss's judgements of her in a recent performance review. Feeling increasingly anxious that if she doesn't show her enthusiasm, she won't get promoted, she interrupts, but her point is mistimed and comes out sounding critical.

To complicate things further, what could be an away move for someone one day might be a toward move for them another day. So, having a couple of glasses of wine with dinner one evening may be a toward move if this action brings you closer to what is important to you at the time, maybe fun, socialising, relaxing or treating yourself. Another evening, drinking the same amount of alcohol could be an away move if it's driven by an urge to avoid something you don't want to feel, like anxiety or sadness.

The key to responding effectively in any situation is to maintain clarity and connection with your values and intentions on a daily basis.

Lynn and Barry's away moves

Lynn and Barry are a couple. A lot of the time their toward and away moves are polar opposites of one another.

Lynn identifies strongly with the do-do, go-go mode. She's always planning ten steps ahead and trying to juggle what seems like a million balls in the air. Her away moves include saying yes to far too many commitments, particularly in her job, where she works long hours and manages multiple tasks, to the extent that her productivity suffers. She works extremely hard, yet is often disillusioned that she doesn't seem to achieve the same degree of success as her colleagues, who, in her view, do not work as hard yet get more good results.

Outside her work hours, Lynn is on a couple of committees, and also volunteers for charitable organisations. While volunteering can be a toward move for some people, these actions have tipped into away move territory for Lynn, as she is filling her time with work of all kinds, and increasingly missing out on social time with her friends and family.

Lynn secretly hopes that her good deeds will not go unnoticed and that her volunteering will help advance her career. She also gets a high from saying yes to things, a feeling of self-importance from being at the heart of the action.

Sooner or later, Lynn comes to realise that she has bitten off more than she can chew. The build-up of the various small things that she has said yes to and volunteered for leads to massive feelings of overwhelm. Even though she's an organised person, she finds herself waking up early in the morning with thoughts of what she has to do running through her mind. She is in a constant state of worry about not fulfilling her huge itinerary, about letting everyone down. Her worry then morphs into resentment against those who demand her time, time she's volunteered in the first place. Lynn frequently feels so trapped and stressed that her chest hurts.

Barry, on the other hand, identifies more strongly with the back away, not today mode. Being around people and on committees, and going to multiple meetings, are Barry's idea of hell. Barry's away moves generally involve him saying no rather than yes to activities and actions that are outside of his comfort zone. An away move he engages in frequently is staying at home to binge on Netflix or reading a variety of news feeds, constantly checking new sites to validate the claims made in the original article he read.

Barry is self-employed and his away moves have an effect on his business. He avoids checking his phone and emails regularly, and often has a lie-in in the mornings having stayed up until 3 a.m. the previous night. He often misses out on networking meetings, even though he needs these to promote his business, and he doesn't update his website and social media business profiles.

Barry generally did well in very structured work environments, but he's been struggling since he went out on his own. While he knows all he needs to know in order to be successful, he finds it extremely difficult to self-promote. The same analytical brain that makes him briliant at what he does works against him as he tries to compare various different options to find the right or best one. He compares but finds it hard to make any decisions, because in truth Barry is terrified of making the wrong one. All this analysing and terror turn into procrastination, which results in Barry watching more Netflix until 3 a.m., and the cycle continues.

Many away moves have short-term gain

While Lynn and Barry's away moves look vastly different, it's important to recognise that they both lead to some short-term gain. For Lynn, whose default is to say yes too often and overschedule her time, the short-term gain was a feeling of self-importance, excitement and initial enthusiasm. For Barry, whose default is to say no to anything that feels uncomfortable or may lead to decision-making, the short-term gain is a sense of relief and getting to avoid decisions.

Many away moves involve long term pain

Each of our away moves gives us a sense of relief or achievement in the short term, but they carry a big price tag further down the line.

For Lynn, the long term pain is a toll on her physical and mental health as she puts her deeper needs on hold in order to satisfy her craving for approval and success. She is constantly on a treadmill that has her so caught up, she doesn't take the time to look after herself. In order to rectify this, she would need to say no to some opportunities and sit with the discomfort of possibly disappointing someone or not achieving a career goal.

For Barry, the long term pain is that he gets increasingly stuck in a cycle of overwhelming hopelessness. Each time he says no to something, it reinforces his belief that he is not able to do these things in the first place, making it even more tempting to say no the next time a similar situation arises.

In order to expand his comfort zone, Barry would need to make one of the decisions he's so afraid of making. He would need to decide to say yes more often, even when there is a possibility that things wouldn't work out the way he wants them to.

Toward moves = the middle path

In its simplest terms, the Power of Small is about making consistent toward moves in the direction of a happy medium. Some of you will need to say yes more, whereas others will need to say no more.

Each yes means you need to say no to something else, and vice versa. For example, the more that Lynn says yes to additional commitments in work and on committees, the more she says no to her own health, wellbeing and relationships. Through exercising her toward moves of saying no more often, she then gets the opportunity to say yes more often to her family, friends and her own health and wellbeing.

Similarly, as Barry says yes more often to new and challenging situations, the more he says no to shying away from decision-making.

Remember the self-care zone

Barry's away moves keep him in his comfort zone. When he starts making toward moves, he's venturing outside that comfort zone, but it's important for him to remember to stay within his self-care zone as he progresses.

Barry has learned that a toward move would be to say

yes more, and having experienced the positive effect of this, his temptation might be to take that action and put it on steroids, saying yes to absolutely everything.

But if he does this, Barry will burn out sooner rather than later, ending up right back where he was in the first place. Toward moves are not about doing the polar opposite of what you do all the time. They are always about taking small, consistent, consciously chosen actions outside of your comfort zone, yet firmly planted within your self-care zone.

So, while Barry begins to say yes to things outside his comfort zone, it would be best for him to choose to say yes to one thing only in a week, and slowly progress from there. Similarly for Lynn, saying no to one little thing at work rather than every little thing is the way forward. Saying no to one small thing gives the message, both to herself and her colleagues, that she *can* say no. Lynn should sit with this knowledge for a while and really feel what that is like from a positive point of view, before making her next toward move.

TODAY'S SMALL STEP

WTF?

For those who are having difficulty identifying whether an action is a toward move or an away move, one of the first things we encourage them to do is to ask themselves 'WTF?' or 'what's the function?' of this behaviour.

Is the step you're about to take likely to be effective in bringing you closer to what's important, or is your intention to get away from something you don't want?

The next time you notice uncertainty and doubt around a decision – whether or not to go to the gym after work, to eat the extra pancake at brunch, or to binge-watch box sets for the weekend – take a moment to pause and connect with your underlying intentions and values. Once you pinpoint what's important to you deep down, ask yourself if this action you're contemplating functions to bring you toward or away from what's important. Practising this simple step increases our power to make more conscious choices in the direction of what's important to us.

7

The Why Behind Our Actions

He who has a 'why' to live for can bear with
almost any 'how'. Friedrich Nietzsche

We are all, every single one of us, goal-setters. The majority of our goals, whether it be a big goal like getting to the top in our careers, or a smaller goal like planning a weekend away, are set in order to either achieve happiness or avoid unwanted emotions such as anxiety or sadness.

Often we set goals without even knowing it. For instance, we might see an advertisement for a product on television, and unbeknownst to us we set a goal to buy that product. On a subconscious level we believe that having that product will bring us happiness.

The goals we set are subject to other influences. Every conversation we partake in, or overhear, every piece of media we consume, has an impact. We see people who have more than us or who are better than us at one thing or another, and that has an impact. We see a photograph of a friend having a great holiday on Facebook, and that has an impact. We cannot help but compare our lives to others and give ourselves a hard time when we believe we are falling short.

The problem with goals

We are often far less likely to follow through on a big goal than a small goal. Rather than living our dreams, we may begin to feel like we're living in a nightmare, constantly reminded of how we're falling short in terms of our targets.

However, it's important to note that it's not just setting big goals that's problematic. Each time you set a small goal and do not follow through and achieve it, your confidence erodes a little more. These goals may be as small as getting out of bed five minutes earlier in the morning, or having a piece of fruit instead of a chocolate bar once a day. But when we fail at these goals consistently over time, it has a cumulative negative effect.

What drives your small goals – whether it's something that really matters, such as your health and wellbeing, or some external comparison, such as wanting to be as good as or better than someone else – has a massive impact on your likelihood of successfully following through.

Toward and away motivations

When most of us go to bed at night we set an alarm clock so that we will get up at a certain time the next morning.

Getting up to go about our daily business, whether it be work, study or otherwise, is a goal we set.

It is possible that this goal could be motivated primarily by away motivation. Away motivation in this case would be turning up for work on time only to avoid adverse consequences, such as getting into trouble, losing your wages or possibly getting fired. The same goal of getting up for work could be the product of toward motivation if the primary desire is to connect with others, or to do work you believe in, or to receive wages because this is important for your health, wellbeing and family.

If you have toward motivation in this scenario, you might still have the thought, 'Oh, I can't believe I have to get up,' when your alarm goes off at 7 a.m. You are only human, after all. However, if your goal of going to work is primarily motivated by toward motivation, your chances of fulfilling your goal are greatly increased. By comparison, away motivation often diminishes your chances of fulfilling your goal.

If you're noticing that you're struggling to follow through on your goals, big or small, it is worth reconnecting with your toward motivation – the why behind the actions you want to take.

Alice's groundhog day

When Alice came to see us first, she was very depressed. Her children had grown up and left home, and two of them had families of their own now. As a wife, mother and grandmother,

Alice felt like she had been adhering to everyone else's idea of how she should be living her life. She believed that she always needed to be kind and generous, even at the expense of her own health and wellbeing. She thought that she should say yes anytime she was asked to mind her grandchildren. She told us that every day felt like groundhog day. She was caught in a loop where she believed other people were dictating what she should and shouldn't be doing.

Alice had fallen into a repetitive cycle of self-defeating behaviour. She would give what she thought others wanted from her until she burned out, and then she would become depressed and withdraw from her family and friends. She would stop answering phone calls and text messages. She would either decline invitations or cancel plans last minute. She would often make goals around staying connected to others and not relapsing into depression; however, she found it incredibly hard to attain them.

When we looked at the idea of toward motivation at the start of our work together, Alice said she had absolutely no idea what her values were, because she had always been guided by the wants and needs of others. Through taking time to connect to how Alice wanted to see herself and how she wanted to be remembered by others, she quickly realised that she did in fact love spending time with her children and grandchildren. She had identified that deep down she held close the values of loving and being loved, and nurturing intimacy in her relationships, and she committed to allowing those to be the guide for her toward moves.

Alice's 5-minute breakout

Alice's 5-minute breakout involved consciously reconnecting, just after breakfast, to her toward motivation underlying the activites that she was engaging in each day. She would visualise her day's activities and notice how these were linked to her core values and what they brought her closer to. At the end of this conscious 5-minute breakout, Alice made a commitment to reconnect with this towards motivation throughout her daily activities, and to reassess the next morning.

As Alice did this, the activities she engaged in started to feel different. She also learned to identify when she was doing things from a place of away motivation. She came to understand that this wasn't good for her or her family, as she was usually acting from a place of resentment.

Now, Alice chooses to spend time with her family out of toward motivation and she balances this with sometimes choosing alone or downtime, also from a place of toward motivation — her desire to take care of herself too. This has had a big impact on her cycle of depression. Alice still has sad moments, but while before they would last for weeks, now they frequently pass in minutes.

TODAY'S SMALL STEP

Toward motivations

In your diary, answer the following questions:

1. What goals would I set if I had nobody left to prove myself to?

2. What goals would I invest my time in achieving if my anxieties, fears or struggles weren't an issue?

3. What goals are so important for me to pursue that I am willing to feel unwanted emotions and accept uncomfortable experiences?

These are your toward motivations.

Once you have identified these, decide on one goal to commit to for the next week. Read this page of your diary every day, reminding yourself of your toward motivations. Watch what impact staying grounded in toward motivation has on achieving your goals.

8

The Power Struggle

Knowing others is intelligence; knowing yourself is true wisdom.
Mastering others is strength; mastering yourself is true power.
Lao Tzu

In previous chapters, we explored how avoiding unwanted experiences is ultimately futile and is often the very thing holding you back. However, while you may not be capable of controlling all aspects of your life, you do have it within you to change the areas where you are giving your power away needlessly. You can also learn how and where to strategically place yourself in your life at any given moment, to make the situation work for you.

Power versus powerless

Essentially, your life is divided into two camps – the parts that you do have power over, and the parts that you are powerless to change.

This distinction is really important to make. The root cause of many mental health conditions can be found in our tendency to put time and energy into trying to control those areas of our lives over which we are powerless.

It is part of our human nature to try and exert power over those areas of our lives that cause us the most discomfort, and we often do this by engaging in away moves.

What You Are Powerless Over (No Choice)	What You Have Power Over (Choice)
Other people's thoughts, feelings, attitudes and actions in the past, present and future Your own thoughts and feelings in the past, present and future Your values, attitudes and actions in the past and future.	Your values, attitudes and actions right this moment

When we show this table to our clients, groups and workshop attendees, they often quickly identify that placing their time and energy in trying to change the past is a way of draining their power. However, sometimes people have a tougher time in identifying how they are powerless over the future. Here is the thing, if you engage in a number of small actions in the present moment, you greatly influence your future in ways that will most likely be beneficial. However, there are of course some aspects of the future that are completely outside of your control in relation to your own health and that of your loved ones and in relation to births, deaths, marriages, separations and the economy.

It is also common to believe that we have more control or power over other people than we actually have. Sure, we can all respond to other people in ways that are most likely going to be helpful and lead to meaningful connections. However, you've probably had enough birthdays to encounter at least one, if not many people who, no matter what you do or don't do, say or don't say, continue to respond to you in ways that you don't like.

It can be hard to get our heads around the fact that we are powerless over our thoughts and emotions in the present moment. Nobody chooses to think anxious, depressed or distressing thoughts or feel unwanted feelings in the first place. However, once we notice that we are having unwanted or distressing thoughts and feelings, we have a choice and power over how to respond to them. When we respond to our unwanted internal experiences in a way that seeks to control or minimise them, we often make them bigger and more distressing in the long term. Whereas, when we notice our unwanted internal experiences in a way that is connected to the present moment and our values, and decide to and redirect our attention to actions that matter to us, we can greatly reduce or mimimise the unwanted impact these thoughts have on us and our lives.

It's an interesting paradox that when we realise and acknowledge that we don't have power over these aspects of our experience in the first place, we can then respond in a way that takes our power back. The key to really embodying the Power of Small is to shift your focus so you engage in a number of small toward moves, one at a time, in areas that you have power over.

Jack's power game

Jack came to see us because he was feeling completely powerless in his life. His ex-girlfriend and mother of his two-year-old daughter had told him to leave the apartment she owned, and he was back living with his parents, sleeping in his old childhood bedroom.

Jack had become a father at a very young age. As a result, he had been torn between family life and the fun and freedom his friends were having. Often the fun and freedom won out. He regularly went partying with his mates, shirked his responsibilities as a partner and parent, both physically and financially, and increasingly behaved as if he was still single.

Jack was already in a situation that he couldn't reverse. He had become a parent when he was not ready for it. The way he tried to control the situation was by pretending on a certain level that it wasn't happening, that he could just go on the way he had before his daughter was born. His power struggle was with the discomfort of having to take responsibility for his child. He tried to wield control over his discomfort by making lots of away moves from it.

When his partner threw him out, Jack was pitched into a sense of further disempowerment. Back living with his parents, he tried to control this distressing situation by spending hours playing computer games during the day and going out with his friends in the evenings. He avoided seeing his ex-partner and daughter, because it felt too painful for him — another away move in an effort to exert control over his discomfort. While on the surface it appeared to those around him that he just didn't care, Jack knew that this couldn't be further from the truth. When he looked at the function of his away moves he discovered they were all attempts to move away from the fear that he wouldn't be a good father. He spent most of his time desperately trying to distract from thoughts that he would mess up and fail his daughter. Although it was painful for him to face up to the very fear he had been running from, Jack was also able to connect with just how important being a good father was to him.

Soon after, Jack came to the conclusion that he wanted to consciously work on building good relationships with his ex-partner and daughter. We helped him to recognise his small away moves from the discomfort of responsibility, and how they had built up to disempower him even further.

Jack's 5-minute breakout

We asked Jack to take five minutes each day to recognise what he did have power over in the here and now, and how he could choose to actively engage in small toward moves right this moment, which would help towards a better relationship with his ex-partner and daughter.

One of these toward moves was so tiny, it might have seemed pointless, but it was the catalyst for a complete change in Jack's life. We asked him to text his ex-partner every second day to ask how his daughter was doing. This simple move not only began to engage Jack with his responsibility in a gentle way, it also gave his ex the message that he was becoming ready to be a reliable father.

We worked with Jack to build up other small toward moves, but it was the consistent texting to enquire about his daughter's welfare that provided the bedrock for him to regain a sense of his power. We are happy to report that although Jack and his ex didn't get back together, his daughter now stays with him in his new apartment every second weekend, and he sees his daughter regularly in the intervening period — remaining on good terms with his ex-partner, in an agreeable co-parenting setup.

Other power struggles

We all have areas of our life in which we feel disempowered, and which we try to control by making away moves from them. For instance, Mary doesn't earn enough money to buy luxuries, so she uses credit cards to do so, thereby controlling the discomfort of not having enough. Her purchases give her a short-term sense of power but create long term disempowerment.

John struggles with asthma. In an effort to comfort himself in this situation over which he feels he has no power, he smokes 20 cigarettes a day, each of them a small, cumulative move away from good health.

A small toward move for Mary might be to make an agreement with herself here and now that she is entitled to one luxury purchase per week that costs no more than €20. A small toward move for John might be to take three minutes to practise mindfulness of his five senses before he smokes each cigarette. Since John usually smokes outside, he deliberately takes three minutes to connect to all he can see, hear, smell, taste and feel. The aim is for John to pay attention to his senses a little as he would have as a younger child – full of curiosity. This helps him to acknowledge any unwanted thoughts and emotions that he may have been trying to avoid through smoking, and also gives him the opportunity to ground himself in a way that is more likely to bring him closer to his value of health.

TODAY'S SMALL STEP

Three steps towards empowerment

The three steps towards empowerment over an uncomfortable area of your life are:

1. Identify an area in your life that you feel powerless over. If one area seems too overwhelming to consider right now, select a specific task, goal or interaction that you struggle with.

2. Identify the short-term actions you take to avoid

the discomfort of feeling powerless and assess their long term pain. Ask yourself, 'What away moves do I make in an effort to control my discomfort that ultimately make me feel more disempowered in the long run?' For example, when Michelle noticed thoughts that she would never be able to lose enough weight or get healthy, she almost immediately reached for junk food to temporarily numb the helplessness and hopelessness she experienced. Or Lynn, who frequently said yes to opportunities to the point of burnout so to avoid the thoughts that she wasn't good enough or that her career would not progress if she turned down offers. In both cases, the impact of these short-term strategies led to more of the same suffering again and again. When they connected with the cost of their power struggle and faced the discomfort they had been unwilling to feel, Michelle and Lynn found the freedom to choose to do things differently.

3. Identify and commit to one tiny action that would pivot your away move into a step towards your values. As clearly as you can, recognise what is most important to you when you reflect on where you feel powerless. What is it that you want your actions to bring you towards? For Lynn it was achieving more balance and security and for Michelle, health, wellbeing and connection. Once you have connected with what is important, choose one toward move you can take and commit to replacing one away move.

Why not try to take these steps today?

9

D.O.T.S.

*No one ever tells us to stop running away from fear . . . the advice
we usually get is to sweeten it up, smooth it over, take a pill, or
distract ourselves, but by all means make it go away.*
Pema Chödrön

There are four strategies that we use to avoid pain in our lives:
distraction, opting out, thinking traps, and self-defeating
actions. Or to put it more succinctly, D.O.T.S.

These strategies are often difficult to look at honestly
and openly, as they tend to involve behaviours that we hide
from others or find difficult to accept in ourselves. They
often feel good, or at the very least less bad, in the short
term, yet almost inevitably result in our feeling worse in
the long term.

A key premise underlying the Power of Small philosophy

is that you are the pilot in your own life, where your experience is the most important gauge of what is workable or unworkable.

So, let's join the D.O.T.S. in your life to see what small actions are working for you, and which are working against you. True power comes from knowing the impact of your actions in the short, medium and long term so that you can make the best-informed decisions at any particular moment.

D is for distraction

Distraction is one of the most common go-to strategies we use in dealing with stress and when we feel overwhelmed. It doesn't help that we are often told to not think about something, or to take our minds off difficulties.

Distraction is any activity we engage in to try to get away from an unwanted mental experience. Classic examples are browsing the internet, obsessively checking smartphones, keeping busy, cleaning, drinking wine or other alcoholic beverages, and consuming sugary, stodgy junk foods.

In the short term, distraction strategies can be very effective, which is why many people are attracted to them. In the long term, however, distraction does nothing to address the core issue. It also takes a lot of conscious effort, making it impossible to maintain over long periods of time without pretty disastrous consequences.

Here is a table of some of the most common types:

Common Distraction Strategies		
Eating sweets and chocolate	Cleaning and organising the house	Looking after the neighbour's children
Social media	Checking emails	Volunteering
Listening to music	Watching TV	Binge-watching Netflix
Browsing the internet	Computer games	Online shopping
Daydreaming	Cigarettes	Alcohol
Drugs	Drinking copious amounts of coffee	Sex
Working long hours	Taking work home	Reading
Online messaging	One-night stands	Pornography
Online dating apps	News	Soap operas
Gym	Running	Leaving the house
E-cigarettes	Texting	Making lists
Online articles	Partying	Phoning friends

O is for opting out

Often distraction and opting out are two sides of the same coin. When we are busy distracting ourselves on the internet, eating chocolate or having a glass, or bottle, of wine, we are almost inevitably avoiding addressing something else, such as our self-care, asserting our needs, or the basics such as healthy eating and exercising. It doesn't help that we are often urged to do what makes you feel good.

Unfortunately, the harsh reality is that a lot of things that are ultimately better for our health and wellbeing in the long term, such as asserting our needs, eating healthily and getting regular exercise, involve at least a partial necessity to feel uncomfortable, at least in the short term.

Opting out is when we avoid people, activities or situations in order to minimise or negate feelings of discomfort. It can include a whole range of actions, including avoiding calls, texts, events, emails, or being assertive. Opting out is very tempting, as it almost always brings at least temporary relief. The moment we opt out, our sense of overwhelm begins to subside and life feels that little bit more manageable.

It's important to remember that every single one of us opts out. This is a normal and natural part of life. You can only really take your power back when you identify the small actions and inactions you engage in on a daily basis, so that you then have the power to choose how to respond.

Here is a table of the most common opting out strategies that we have noticed in others, and ourselves:

Common Opting Out Strategies		
Avoiding exercise	Not eating healthily	Not paying bills on time
Cancelling appointments concerning your own wellbeing if asked to do something for someone else	Putting off texting or calling people back when overwhelmed	Not doing exercises recommended by health professionals
Avoiding dating	Avoiding parties	Avoiding leaving the house
Not initiating contact with friends	Not going on holidays or taking breaks	When looking for a job, avoiding making applications
Avoiding looking for jobs	Putting friends off meeting when they initiate contact	Avoiding intimacy
Not asking for help when struggling	Not expressing emotions	Avoiding people or relationships where there are high levels of emotions, especially anger or sadness

Avoiding spending time with family and attending family events	Not telling others about depression or anxiety	Avoiding smear testing
Avoiding confrontation	Avoiding asking for something that might put someone else out	Avoiding people who are challenging
Avoiding events that you believe will cause anxiety	Avoiding working on a creative project	Avoiding going for promotions
Avoiding telling people how you feel	Avoiding leaving a relationship that isn't working	Avoiding staying at home on your own
Avoiding public transport	Avoiding aeroplanes	Avoiding travelling alone
Staying busy	Daydreaming	Excessive worrying

T is for thinking traps

Whereas thoughts are generally strings of words that appear in our minds, over which we have little or no control (such as the thought, 'I'm not good enough'), thinking traps are how we respond to such ideas, for example by falling into the washing machine trap, where thoughts go round and round the same trajectory: catastrophising, challenging the thoughts, suppressing them, or engaging in positive thinking.

Every day we get messages via the media (both traditional

and social) about how we should think – that we should 'just think positively', that we will be happier, healthier and ultimately more productive if we can just think right. We often get caught up in one of these thinking traps, which often causes us more harm than good in the long run.

Here is a table of common thinking traps:

Common Thinking Traps		
Washing machine thinking – going over the same thoughts again and again	Blinkered thinking – becoming completely blinkered by your thoughts	Pink elephant thinking – trying really hard not to think your thoughts
Catastrophising – becoming blinkered by the worst possible outcomes	Positive thinking – trying to think of positive thoughts instead	Challenging thinking – trying to challenge your thoughts

S is for self-defeating actions

There are numerous ways in which we can unwittingly become reliant on an action to help us avoid a certain feeling in the short term. Over-reliance on food, caffeine and prescription medications are just some of the self-defeating actions we witness. Self-defeating actions include any actions that cause us more pain in the long term.

Some self-defeating actions are primarily driven by our desire to avoid a particular emotion. For example, someone who doesn't like conflict might push down their feelings until they eventually explode and contribute to an even bigger conflict as a result. Other self-defeating actions might be primarily motivated by a desire to avoid a specific behaviour. For example, someone may avoid healthy eating or exercising even though they have a heart problem. We want to pay special attention to anything you do that has a particularly unfavourable impact on your life.

Here is a table of common self-defeating strategies:

Common Self-Defeating Strategies		
Overindulging in sugary and stodgy foods	Ingesting foods and drinks, even when you have an intolerance or allergy	Staying up too late
Staying in bed too long	Missing deadlines	Procrastinating
Cancelling on friends and loved ones at the last minute	Lashing out at loved ones	Not asserting needs on an ongoing basis
Pushing yourself too hard	Going back into training before an injury heals	Undersleeping (ie sleeping under six hours)

Overworking	Saying yes to too many things, to the point of burnout	Drinking too much alcohol
Ending relationships to avoid vulnerability	Lying to loved ones on an ongoing basis	Isolating yourself
Cutting yourself	Pulling hair out	Getting too many unhealthy takeaways
Avoiding medical and psychological help	Taking drugs	Staying in a job that drains all energy
Unsafe sex	Jumping from one intimate relationship to the next	Not asking for help

Joining the D.O.T.S.

When we face our demons head on it can feel very painful, at least in the short term. However, if you recognised any of the strategies above and understand that you use them, you can begin to get a clearer picture of how you are dealing with life. Through this process comes empowerment.

With that empowerment in mind, it's time to look at all the small ways that you deliberately or unconsciously try to control, minimise or manipulate your internal experiences, and how these strategies work for or against you.

Here are three questions to ask yourself:

1. Have any of your own small D.O.T.S. strategies permanently got rid of your unwanted internal experiences (thoughts, emotions, memories, bodily sensations)?

2. In general, when you use these small D.O.T.S. strategies rigidly or excessively, do they make your unwanted internal experiences better or worse?

3. When you use these small D.O.T.S. strategies rigidly or excessively, do you move closer to who and where you want to be, or further away?

We asked Michelle, one of our case studies, these three questions and here is how she responded.

1. Have any of your own small D.O.T.S. strategies permanently got rid of your unwanted internal experiences (thoughts, emotions, memories, bodily sensations)?

Michelle's answer was the inevitable no. If any of these strategies could permanently get rid of her unwanted internal experiences, chances are she wouldn't have been seeking help. We are guessing that the same is true for you; if there was a strategy that permanently got rid of unwanted internal experiences while simultaneously moving you closer to your values, chances are you wouldn't be reading this book now.

No one has ever found a strategy that permanently gets rid of their unwanted internal experiences. The path to reclaiming our power is in taking small steps towards being able to sit with them, which inevitably changes our relationship with them – and enables us to begin making better choices, from a place of acceptance.

This realisation really helped Michelle. For years, she had thought that there was something fundamentally flawed or broken within her because she hadn't found the one magical skill or strategy that would permanently get rid of her unwanted internal experiences. To recognise that her struggle was a shared and inevitable one helped her build a sense of compassion. We hope this will happen for you too.

2. In general, when you use these small D.O.T.S. strategies rigidly or excessively, do they make your unwanted internal experiences better or worse?

Michelle recognised that most of her strategies generally made her feel better in the short term, but much worse in the long term. For example, when she ate sugar and stodgy foods after a rough day at work, she would often get a temporary reprieve from her mind repeating the events of the day on an endless spin cycle. However, pretty quickly once she stopped eating, she started to feel a whole lot worse about herself. And the more she adopted these small strategies, the bigger the problem became for her.

It's important to validate how normal and natural it is to engage in D.O.T.S. strategies. It is part of our humanity. We all want to feel good rather than bad, yet research shows us that the less willing we are to feel something, the more we will actually feel it. So the less willing I am to feel sadness, the more likely I am to experience depression. This is a depressing fact, yet an important one to realise – we actually give emotions our power by trying to control them. An emotion can never control us without us inadvertently giving it our power.

As you ask yourself these questions, it is useful to remember that we have collectively asked thousands of people the same questions, including Michelle and now you. And we have never met a single person who doesn't experience an adverse impact on their unwanted internal experiences in the long term when they turn to their D.O.T.S. strategies rigidly and excessively. So, if this is the case for you, please know that it is a widespread experience.

3. When you use these small D.O.T.S. strategies rigidly or excessively, do you move closer to who and where you want to be, or further away?

The answer for Michelle was further away. When she engaged in small actions with the aim of moving further away from unwanted mental experiences, not only did she exacerbate the unwanted mental experiences, she also moved further away from the life that matters to her. So, for example, when she binged on sugary foods, paid excessive fees for a new gym membership and then didn't attend, or avoided meeting friends in a rigid and excessive way to put off feelings of sadness and anxiety, she inevitably moved much further away from who and where she wanted to be.

Again, Michelle's experience is pretty typical of what we

have witnessed whenever we've asked this question. So many of us fall into the trap of short-term gain, long term pain. In the next parts of the book we'll show you a number of compassionate ways to change your relationship with your unwanted internal experiences so that you can move closer to who and where you want to be, one small, manageable step at a time.

TODAY'S SMALL STEP

Join your D.O.T.S. and connect to the cost

Have a look through the lists of common distractions, opting out, thinking and self-defeating actions. Identify as many strategies as possible that you engage in under each heading. Then ask yourself the three questions above to see how little or how much your small D.O.T.S. actions have given you power or taken your power away. It can be tempting to skip over this step and move straight to focusing on the toward moves. Indeed, we have got caught in this trap ourselves. However, in our experience and in the research, it has been found that the more fully you connect with and acknowledge the costs of your away moves in a compassionate way, the more motivated you are to engage in toward moves. We have a lot of toward moves for you to engage in during Part Two.

It's important to acknowledge that asking yourself these questions will likely bring up some unwanted thoughts, emotions and bodily sensations. This is a natural part of the process. As best you can, acknowledge these thoughts, emotions and bodily sensations as they arise within you, without attempting to change them in any way. You may find it helpful to make a note of them in your small steps diary, or to simply name and acknowledge your unwanted internal experiences without engaging in a struggle against them. As you will see increasingly in the next parts of the book, it is not these unwanted internal experiences that are your enemy, but rather your many attempts to control, minimise or avoid them.

Part Two

From the
Inside Out

10
The Rules of Engagement

The hardest challenge is to be yourself in a world where everyone is trying to make you be somebody else.
EE Cummings

Like a fish in a pond, whether we are aware of it or not, we are immersed in the culture we live in, and we cannot exist outside of that culture. This unavoidable environment feeds us the rules we need in order to fit in and function in the world. And so, for instance, we learn the things we need to express and suppress in order to fit into the socially accepted roles within society. And we learn to follow the rules and demands of these roles, for example, what it means to be a good friend or family member, or how to behave in order to be considered a good person.

In our work, we consistently see issues stemming from this pressure to conform, among clients who are feeling stuck or overwhelmed. Very often they are trapped in a loop, constantly making decisions according to internalised rules around what a good life looks like.

The happiness rule

We've internalised certain rules, mostly from the messages we received about the world and ourselves as we were growing up. One of these rules is that happiness is the normal state for people to be in, and therefore if you're not happy, you must be defective, broken or a failure.

In reality it is healthy and natural to feel a broad range of emotions, which are determined by whatever is going on in our lives at a particular time. It is also unrealistic and even unhelpful to be happy in all circumstances, as there are times when it is not warranted. It is more natural to feel anger, disgust, fear and sadness, for example, in response to an unwanted event than it is to experience happiness, calmness or excitement. Whether something major happens such as losing a job, or we simply have a bad day, a combination of these unwanted emotions is the natural state for humans. We usually experience overwhelm when we have a combination of anger, disgust, fear and sadness at a level that feels unbearable for us.

Many people live by the rule that they should not feel sad, anxious or overwhelmed and that they have to get rid of these feelings in order to enjoy a better life. Ironically, it is this belief that often results in us demonising unwanted thoughts and feelings, which often exacerbates them further.

When we lead groups and workshops, the vast majority of

participants have, at some level, bought into this happiness rule. And far from the rule helping them to feel wanted emotions more often and unwanted emotions less often, they experience the opposite. Often when they're experiencing an unwanted emotion, such as sadness or anxiety, they go into their heads to try and get rid of it and berate themselves for feeling it. This actually fuels the unwanted emotion further and blinds them to aspects of the present moment that could bring a sense of joy or calm.

On the flipside, often when group participants feel a wanted emotion, such as happiness or calmness, they try to figure out how to keep feeling this way. Of course, this is totally understandable, particularly if someone has been struggling with depression or anxiety. Why wouldn't they want some relief? However, this attempt to hold onto wanted emotions generally drives them straight into anxiety, and the positive emotion has disappeared far quicker than if they simply allowed themselves to notice it and embrace it in the moment.

The antidote to getting caught up in the happiness rule is to practise self-acceptance. Self-acceptance does not mean that you need to like, love or want unwanted emotions. However, it does ask that you acknowledge whatever emotions arise as understandable given your unique life history. Little by little, you can practise treating yourself with the same kindness as you'd extend to others in a similar scenario. Those who attend our groups and workshops are often surprised by the major impact these small changes have on their lives. They are able to connect more fully to their loved ones and can enjoy life so much more when they are not constantly trying to control what emotions they will feel.

The shoulds and musts

In each small decision we make on a daily basis, if we stop to consider our choice, there are usually a few shoulds and musts that show up.

Such rules include 'you should always be polite', or 'you must always tell the truth', or 'you should always respect your elders/boss/parent'. There is nothing wrong with these rules per se, but if they rigidly affect what you do and don't do to the extent that you lose contact with who you are, they become problematic.

For example, the person who buys into a rule about being polite may constantly go along with what everyone else wants for fear of upsetting or offending them. They then become increasingly disillusioned and passive, letting anger and resentment fester within them.

Or the person who believes you must always speak your mind may give feedback even when it is not warranted, which may cause issues in their work or social life. Whenever one believes that they should always respect a particular category of people, they run the risk of not responding effectively when these people act in harmful ways towards them.

Our shoulds and musts are often very useful. Instead of having to think on our feet in unfamiliar situations, we can refer to a previously stored template of similar scenarios to help us to navigate the current predicament. Using these rules, we adjust our behaviour to fit the situation we find ourselves in.

However, when we live our lives according to the shoulds and musts without question, we forget to trust our own needs, desires and instincts. And if we live our lives overly focused on not breaking the rules, our authentic desires constantly need to be quietened and suppressed.

When we persistently live by these rules, we're trying to be in control. We want to control the outcomes of our actions; we're seeking comforting outcomes and avoiding uncomfortable ones. But we can only operate like this for so long before we lose a sense of ourselves and disconnect from what's important to us.

Most of the time these rules act as helpful signposts across a variety of complex situations and relationships. But a rule becomes problematic when you rigidly cling to it as a one size fits all approach, even when acting by it harms you, or stops you from achieving what you need from the situation.

Flexible guidelines

Before you can begin to make the changes you desire, you need to look at how you are becoming caught up in rules, and question if they are working for you so that you're getting what you want out of life.

Once we become aware of how our decisions are being influenced by the rules, we can start challenging them one by one.

For instance, if you notice that you get caught up in the rule that you have to keep people happy, you can start to acknowledge how this rule is impacting your actions and inactions. Perhaps you don't tell people when you're upset and you allow this to fester and boil up, until eventually you let fly at someone. You might also constantly settle for less than what you want, because you're afraid of rocking the boat and of others disapproving of your choices.

A good way to break out of a rule is to find a new, flexible guideline instead, which takes both yourself and others into account. First acknowledge whether your rule about keeping others happy is determined by toward motivation or away motivation. (Very often when we hold on rigidly to our rules, they are determined by away motivation.) Then find your toward motivation – how you want to respond to others – and create a new flexible guideline rather than a rule.

For example, frequently the motivation behind a rigid rule such as 'I must keep people happy' is really about not wanting others to be disappointed with you, or not wanting to feel some unwanted emotion, such as sadness. When you connect with the toward motivation underlying how you want to keep others happy, you may realise that you want to treat people with compassion or respect.

This toward motivation allows you a lot more flexibility. From here you can give yourself the guideline that you will respond to others in a way that is respectful, even when you don't necessarily agree with them, and at the same time be respectful and compassionate to yourself.

Previously, if a partner did something that upset you, such as forgot an anniversary, under the old rule of 'I must keep people happy' you may have pushed down your disappointment. However, with the new, more flexible guideline you could tell your partner that you were upset in a way that is respectful and understanding of their particular circumstances, such as being busy at work or having too much on their mind. In speaking up for your own disappointment in a compassionate way, you will also be respecting your own feelings.

TODAY'S SMALL STEP

Does living by rules bring you towards or away from who you want to be?

Write the heading 'Rules I Live By' at the top of a fresh page in your small steps diary. Divide the page into left and right. On the left write down three cultural rules that you live by. We are often living by these rules without even being aware of them, so it might take some thinking before you come up with three. Stay focused, knowing that you actually live by many cultural rules. You can use some of the examples outlined in this chapter as a prompt.

Acknowledging your rules and writing them down is the first important step towards breaking free from something that may be holding you back from the life you truly want to live.

On the right-hand side of the page, write down a more flexible guideline for each of the rules, to guide your actions going forward. Use the example in this chapter of moving from the rule 'I must keep people happy' to 'I choose to treat people with compassion and respect' as inspiration.

11
The Risk of Relationships

Because true belonging only happens when we present our authentic, imperfect selves to the world, our sense of belonging can never be greater than our level of self-acceptance. Brené Brown

From the moment we are born, whether we like it or not, we cannot exist alone. We come into the world primed to connect with others and instinctively we focus our attention on our primary caregiver, usually our mother, who not only feeds us so that we can stay alive, but bonds with us so our emotional selves can be nurtured. Connection is essential for survival.

We don't just stop needing connection, both social and emotional, as adults. A recent meta-analysis combining a large number of research studies found that isolation was as detrimental to a person's health and wellbeing as smoking 15 cigarettes a day, or being obese.

However, the world has become increasingly individualised. People are more and more isolated. We have never had more means of connecting to others, through texts, emails, smartphones and computer applications, but research about our internet and social media habits indicates that many of us are lonelier than ever.

Perhaps it's not surprising then that most of our behaviours are driven by the need to avoid social exclusion. We do this by trying to gain social approval in both big and small ways. One recent research study conducted in Ireland shows that over half of Irish workers lie about how they spend their weekends. When asked by co-workers, many exaggerated or fabricated what they did on those days, as they didn't want to appear boring.

The fear factor

In our practice, we have worked with many people who are afraid to share their actual experiences, or their thoughts and feelings on a topic, for fear of being rejected or inciting anger. The vast majority of us are like this to some extent. It can be as small as going to one movie when your friend suggests it, when you'd really rather go to a different one, and you move away from your true want without stating your preference. Or the stakes can be considerably higher, where you are constantly in a cycle of pushing down your own feelings in order to placate those of a partner, friend or work colleague.

One or two small incidents like this are unlikely to have a

major impact on your overall wellbeing and quality of life. However, it's worth remembering that each small away move adds up, and this begins to have a huge effect on the direction you are heading in your life. Needless to say, when you are consistently not being true to yourself, you start feeling like a fraud, and often become more and more disconnected from others.

Four small moves towards authenticity in relationships

1. Sharing what your preference would be for an activity, e.g. going to a particular café that you like

2. If you are feeling anxious or down, instead of pretending that everything is fine, simply sharing how you are really feeling

3. Sharing an opinion you have, even if you believe it could be different to that of the person you are speaking to

4. Gently letting someone know when they say something that upsets or offends you

Control issues

An equally problematic trap that we fall into is our desire to control others. We are particularly prone to falling into this trap when it comes to partners, family members and friends.

This may also happen with work colleagues, particularly if you assume a leadership role.

Have you ever thought, 'If only X was different, then I'd be fine.' Some examples of this might be:

1. Mary thinks that if only her son wasn't playing so many computer games and paid more attention in school, then she'd be able to stop worrying about him and enjoy life.

2. Anne thinks that if only her boyfriend was more organised around their shared apartment, she'd be able to function much better.

3. John believes that if only his assistant was more prompt and precise in his work, he'd be able to leave work on time and be happier with his wife and children.

4. Declan thinks that if only his wife would learn to control her anger issues, their relationship would be perfect.

The vast majority of us can get caught up in this trap; we hinge our own happiness and wellbeing on what another person does or does not do.

There are a number of ways in which we respond to others when we're trying to change their behaviour or control their actions. We might be snappy or passive-aggressive when they do something that displeases us. Or perhaps when they finally do what we asked them to do, rather than thanking them or acknowledging it, we only point out how long it took them to follow through. There are a number of ways in which we respond to others when we're trying to change their behaviour.

More often than not, these attempts to control someone else may result in some short-term gain. Perhaps the other person does what you want and you get a temporary feeling of relief. However, this short-term gain usually comes with the price tag of long term pain. This person may become more and more distant from you, and they might even start deliberately doing the opposite of what they know you want them to do. Nobody likes feeling they are being manipulated or controlled.

Four small moves towards letting go of trying to control others

1. Step into their shoes. If you find yourself in an argument, step back for one moment and gently ask yourself if you might be wrong, or if the other person might have a point. Try to step into their point of view, and witness things from their perspective.

2. Delegate an action. Try and trust that someone else can do a small job just as well as you can, and allow them to do it without interfering. Praise them when it is done, even if it is not up to your standards.

3. Try a no advice policy with someone in your life. Simply listen to their problems and tell them you understand, resisting the urge to try and fix it for them.

4. Allow someone else to make the choice. Call a friend and suggest going out for dinner. Ask them to choose where you will go.

We cannot try to control others without it negatively impacting our relationships. We also cannot protect ourselves from other people unless we shut them out completely and keep them at a distance. In order to make room for the relationships we want, we need to make room for the risk that we will experience disappointment, loss, rejection, shame and all the other messy stuff that relationships come packaged in.

TODAY'S SMALL STEP

My toward moves in relationships

In your small steps diary, write at the top of a page, 'My Toward Moves in Relationships'. Now identify whether needing to practise more authenticity in relationships, or letting go of control in relationships, is more important for you to work on right now.

Identify just one small toward move that you will commit to over the next couple of days. You can adapt one of the examples given to identify the most meaningful toward move for you to engage in right now.

Now write down one toward motivation for your toward move, which will increase your chances of following through. For example:

Toward move: I will ask myself if I am wrong in arguments.

Toward motivation: I want to have a more equal relationship, rather than a resentful one.

12
Mind Games

I used to think that the brain was the most wonderful organ in my body. Then I realised who was telling me this. Emo Philips

We often take what our minds tell us as gospel. We say things like, 'I just wouldn't be able for that', or 'that just wouldn't be me', to justify backing out of actions that may very well bring us closer to who and where we want to be. We frequently make a call about whether we should or shouldn't do something based on what our mind tells us in the moment, rather than on our actual lived experience and what matters to us.

This is because of our survival instinct – our minds are literally trying to keep us safe. However, following the safe mind can lead to an overwhelmingly unfulfilling, uneventful life at one end of the spectrum, or an overwhelmingly overscheduled and unmanageable life at the other.

We often get variations of the following advice when we're going through a difficult time: Just don't think about it. Don't worry. Think positive. However, it is not that easy, and indeed not always possible. Some unwanted thoughts stick with us, and keep coming back.

Your mind, left unchecked, is unlikely to lead you to a rich, full, meaningful life. It is far more likely to tempt you into a whole host of away moves that keep you within your comfort zone and repeating the same cycles that have you feeling overwhelmed in the first place.

Four thinking traps

There are a few key thinking traps that many of us fall into:

1. **The pink elephant trap**

   Take a moment and bring a vision of a pink elephant into your mind's eye. Now take another moment and try not to think about the pink elephant. How did you get on? Chances are that pink elephant is still on your mind.

   Research shows that the more we try to suppress or push down small thoughts, the bigger they become. So, what happens when you try not to think about the small thought, 'I'm overwhelmed'? You've probably guessed it. You go into overwhelm central. The more you try not to think a small thought, the bigger it gets.

2. **The blinkered trap**

   When a horse is blinkered, its view of the world is
   greatly impaired. And so is yours when you become
   blinkered by your thoughts. Your view of yourself,
   others and the world around you is filtered through
   the thought that you are blinkered by.

   So, for example, if you are blinkered by the
   thought, 'I'm overwhelmed', all of your decisions
   and actions are likely to be chosen in line with this
   belief. As you can imagine, you tend to engage in
   more away moves than toward moves when this is
   the case.

3. **The washing machine trap**

   This trap is commonly called rumination. It's kind
   of like having all your unwanted thoughts swirling
   around and around in an endless washing machine
   cycle. When you're caught in this trap, you often
   buy into the belief that paying this much attention
   to your thoughts will help you be prepared 'just in
   case'. However, the reality is that this trap robs you
   of joy and connection in the present.

4. **The deep-end trap**

   If you try to face your most overwhelming thoughts
   head on, there may be just too much to deal with
   and you could fall into the deep-end trap, where
   your thoughts will be a tangled, overwhelmed mess.
   To stay out of the deep end, you need to take small,

consistent steps to have the biggest impact, while taking care of your mental health at the same time. Doing too much too soon actually sets you up for failure.

TODAY'S SMALL STEP

One small way to get out of a thinking trap

A small yet effective way to break out of a thinking trap is to put the phrase, 'I'm having the thought that . . .' before your thought. For example, if you are blinkered by the thought, 'I'm overwhelmed', try saying, thinking or writing, 'I'm having the thought that I'm over-whelmed.' This puts you at a small remove from the emotion that comes with the thought that you are overwhelmed by, and as a result changes the dynamic of the relationship with that thought. When we separate ourselves from our thought processes, we begin to take our place as observer rather than subject, the 'who' of the opening quote of this chapter – subtly reinforcing the truth that we are not our thoughts. There is relief to be found in the space between our deepest being – our conscious self – and the thoughts that mill around our mind.

13

Wanted and Unwanted Emotions

Sorrow and joy are woven inextricably together. When we distract ourselves from the reality of loss, we also distract ourselves from the beauty, creativity, and mystery of this ever-changing world.

Tara Brach

Given our human tendency to seek pleasure and avoid pain, it makes sense that we seek out some emotions and avoid others. Those emotions we consider 'positive' include happiness, calmness, excitement and curiosity, while those we tend to avoid and consider 'negative' include sadness, anger, frustration, guilt, shame, disappointment, anxiety and agitation.

You don't have to be a mathematician to see that we have considerably more emotions that we consider negative. In fact, Dr Russ Harris, in his bestseller *The Happiness Trap*, says we have twice as many unwanted emotions as we do wanted ones.

Unwanted emotions are neither good nor bad

A small shift that can make a huge difference in your life is to start labelling your emotions as wanted or unwanted, rather than positive or negative. If you view some emotions as positive while branding others as negative, you will be in a lifelong battle against them. And if you are pushing against your emotions, trying to manipulate and change them, you are essentially putting your time and energy into fighting against yourself.

Meanwhile, when you get caught up in this pattern you inevitably start to feel exhausted, as your time, energy and resources are consumed by a self-defeating mission.

In reality, it would be impossible to live a full and vital life unless you were willing to experience some unwanted emotions. If something unwanted happens to you, such as the loss of a job or a relationship, it is more natural to feel sad or angry or disappointed than to feel happy or excited or calm.

The Power of Small approach says that it is not the emotion itself that is the problem. Rather, it is the various small ways in which we respond to our emotions that either give us power over ourselves, or give the emotion power over us.

Whether an unwanted emotion has power over us is determined by the away moves and toward moves we make in situations that cause unwanted emotions to flare up. Here are some examples of away moves and toward moves you might make within what we have termed the SEAT grid:

Situation	Emotion	Away Move	Toward Move
Being bullied in the workplace	Sadness, anger	Pushing down feelings, withdrawing into the self	Asserting needs in work, seeking support of loved ones outside work
Relationship break-up	Sadness, regret	Overly contacting ex-partner or withdrawing from situations that remind you of ex	Balancing acknowledging sadness and staying connected with friends
Partner isn't doing their fair share	Anger disappointment	Making passive-aggressive comments or getting overly angry/blaming	Asserting needs in a compassionate yet firm way

| Falling behind on deadlines | Regret, guilt | Getting lost in distractions, such as social media, or fixating on deadlines at a cost to health | Planning and structuring time to work at optimal level; planning downtime too |
| Fighting within family | Sadness, frustration | Taking sole responsibility for sorting family issues, or avoiding family completely | Recognising what is inside and outside your control; doing what you can and having compassion for your limits |

So, it is not the unwanted emotions that make our lives either better or worse, it is the series of small actions we engage in after an unwanted situation, and unwanted emotions, arise. The Power of Small approach is all about choosing the small short-term pain so that we can enjoy the bigger long term gain.

A way to help you apply this in your life is to remind yourself that all unwanted situations will bring up at least some unwanted emotion. However, if you respond to this situation and the corresponding emotion with an away move you are out at SEA. When you are out at sea, without an adequate map or direction, you can begin to feel stuck and aimless.

However, if you respond with a toward move, you are SET. When you are set you will still most likely feel unwanted emotions, but now you have a map and you have a direction. This will often bring some solace and a sense of purpose amid the challenging situation and corresponding emotions.

TODAY'S SMALL STEP

SEAT grid

In your small steps diary draw a grid, with eight squares, as outlined here. Identify a situation in your life that gives rise to unwanted emotions. As best you can, acknowledge what your default away move is in this situation. Then think of a toward move that may give you some short-term pain, but have the pay-out of long term gain. Over the next week, check in once a day for a couple of minutes and ask yourself are you SET, or at SEA. If you notice you're aimlessly at SEA, reconnect with and engage in your toward move. Then you'll be all SET.

Situation	Emotion	Away Move	Toward Move
Being bullied in the workplace	Sadness, anger	Pushing down feelings, withdrawing from loved ones	Asserting needs in work, seeking support of loved ones outside work

14
Emotion Control

*You can close your eyes to the things you don't want to see, but
you can't close your heart to the things you don't want to feel.*
Unknown

As a society, we have become obsessed with wanting to feel
good, all of the time. We are bombarded with advertisements
for products and services that give the promise of happiness,
while at the same time taking away our feelings of sadness
and anxiety. More and more of us are becoming addicted to
the small endorphin rush of getting a Facebook comment,
a Twitter follower, an Instagram like. We curate images of
ourselves on social media so that we are seen to be always
happy, while following people who do the same.

It's no wonder that many of us are caught up in a perpetual
loop of trying to feel happier in order to consider ourselves
good enough. The moment we feel some unwanted emotion,
a red alert system is activated in our brains, telling us

'something must be wrong!' When we notice this, one small shift would be to acknowledge the thought that something must be wrong, and then ask ourselves what we could do to improve the situation.

The research is really clear in terms of the relationship between our willingness to feel unwanted emotions, such as anxiety and sadness, and our likelihood of experiencing a clinically diagnosable condition such as depression or anxiety disorder. The more we avoid unwanted emotions, the more likely we are to experience anxiety or depression.

It is a powerful fact that it is not sadness or anxiety that are the problem, but the small and varied ways in which we try to *avoid* sadness and anxiety.

Anna's red alert

Anna came to see us because she struggled with anxiety and this struggle was starting to take up the vast majority of her time. She had become totally preoccupied with her anxiety, constantly reading about its negative impact on her body and psychological wellbeing. She wanted rid of it.

Anna went into full-on red alert mode whenever she felt anxious. Her mind would register her anxiety and then quickly start churning out a number of different stories about how dangerous anxiety was for her health. She'd start frantically trying to find ways to get rid of the anxiety, for fear that it was a sign that things were really wrong in her life.

It is important to know that it was not the anxiety itself that became problematic for Anna, but more so the red alert system that was activated in her brain, launching her into threat and survival mode on an ongoing basis. We need this red alert system to alert us to dangers; however, when this mode of being is overly on, we may run into trouble. Anna was internally responding as if she was physically in danger. Neuroimaging studies have confirmed that we can respond to what we perceive as psychological threat, in this case anxiety, in the same way that we respond to a physical threat, such as someone hitting us.

We started to break down the process of Anna's anxiety into small stages. At the beginning, when she felt anxious, she tried really hard to get rid of the feeling, but because she couldn't, this led to anxiety on top of anxiety. At this stage Anna's emotions were a combination of sad, angry, disappointed and overwhelmed.

We asked Anna what she felt when she battled against the unwanted emotions of sadness, anger, disappointment and overwhelm. She said that at this point she was likely to feel hopeless, depressed and ashamed, as if she was a failure.

The more Anna tried to change her emotions around anxiety, the more they grew and developed into a much bigger and complex set of emotions, to the extent that it affected her overall mood and how she went about her daily life.

Anna was overly concerned about what she had heard were the negative aspects of stress and anxiety, but was unaware of their helpful aspects.

Research shows that there are considerable positive

outcomes from stress and anxiety. In her bestselling book, *The Upside of Stress*, Dr Kelly McGonigal shared that those who see stress as a positive thing are more likely to live the longest, healthiest lives. The reality is that we all need stress in order to survive. We need a certain level of stress to get ourselves out of bed in the mornings; we need stress to motivate us to know when something needs to be changed.

Stress can be a great ally if you learn how to respond to it. Recognising and naming the unwanted emotions triggered by a stressful situation is a good start.

Anna's 5-minute breakout

Anna made the following 5-minute breakout part of her morning routine. She would sit upright with her hands in her lap, close her eyes and breathe in and out deeply four or five times.

Anna would then engage in the 'say yes to an unwanted emotion' exercise, which is outlined in today's small step at the end of this chapter. Through this exercise, Anna was able to break out of her default way of relating to her unwanted emotions from a place of pushing them down automatically. The more she practised, the more she realised that when she responded to her unwanted emotions from a place of resistance and avoidance, the bigger those unwanted emotions got. Conversely, when Anna responded to them from a place of letting them be – which was challenging, particularly at the start – the more peaceful she felt in the long term.

Let them be

Research indicates that our emotions come and go within approximately 90 seconds when we allow them to be as they are without trying to change or manipulate them in some way. Ironically, by trying to make our emotions smaller, or less intense, we actually make them bigger and more overwhelming.

If you'd like to change your relationship with unwanted emotions, acknowledge that there is a positive aspect to every one of them. Similar to the thinking traps we outlined earlier, you can also get caught up in a cycle when you try to avoid or change your unwanted emotions. Instead, practise noticing your emotions as they are and letting them be.

In the rest of this book you'll find a variety of different small skills and strategies to help you overcome the common thinking and emotion traps. The underlying approach is essentially the same in each strategy. We need to recognise when we are either over-identifying with, or overly avoiding, our unwanted internal experiences, and then take one small step towards the self-compassionate middle path.

TODAY'S SMALL STEP

Say yes to an unwanted emotion

Is there a situation or a person in your life bothering you at the moment? Think of it (or them), and as best you can, and register the emotion you feel as a result of the thought.

For instance, you might be worried about money. The emotion you register when you think about your lack of money might be fear.

Now, instead of attempting to change how you are feeling, say yes to the emotion. It's important to acknowledge that saying yes to an unwanted emotion does not mean that you like, love or want it, but that you are willing to acknowledge the feeling without trying to get rid of it.

Take a breath and allow yourself to feel it for a moment. Don't try to push it down or change it. Just acknowledge it, and then get on with your day, letting your values be your guide, rather than your emotions.

Maybe you could try this very simple exercise a few times over the coming days. See how it feels to say yes to small, unwanted emotions.

15

Recognise Your Internal Characters

The most fundamental aggression to ourselves, the most fundamental harm we can do to ourselves, is to remain ignorant by not having the courage and the respect to look at ourselves honestly and gently. Pema Chödrön

We are all constantly talking to ourselves. Each of us has one brain, yet it's like we have a number of persistent little voices within us that all have an opinion on what we should and should not be doing. We run into trouble when these small voices start to take on a protagonist role in our lives. In small yet consistent ways, if we just take these internalised characters at face value, without checking in with our values and our toward moves, our life can become more about damage control than meaningful living.

These small characters are based on the messages given to us by our role models over the years and internalised, and on the big and small events that have shaped us. Our internal characters are not necessarily bad. Each one of them serves some key evolutionary function of trying to protect us in some way.

The language that these different internal characters use is very important. What they say and how they say it subtly shapes how we understand and make sense of others and ourselves. For instance, the way we talk to ourselves about mental health, if held as absolute truth, shapes how we behave, for example, – 'I have depression', 'I cannot get out of bed', 'I am overwhelmed with sadness'.

The words and phrases we use to describe our experiences also exert a subtle influence that often takes us out of ourselves and away from our power: 'I was beside myself with worry', 'I could have kicked myself for saying something so silly', 'I just wasn't myself at all this evening'. Power is gained or lost in terms of how we respond to these internalised characters on a daily basis, and as we'll show, it's the small actions that count.

What the characters say

Our internal characters can be broken down into a finite number of types, and they are all instantly recognisable, as is what they tell us.

THE INNER CRITIC

The inner critic has extremely high standards and it most certainly wants to hold you to them, no matter what the cost. She tends to use extreme all-or-nothing language, saying things such as 'you really are not very good at what you do', or 'you'll never get a great job as long as you're so incompetent', or 'you are so far behind, you might as well give up now', or 'this is typical of you, you never learn'. The inner critic knows your weak points and exploits them.

When we become overly influenced by the inner critic, we may engage in a number of small away moves. For some of us, this will involve being so daunted by the big picture that we stick our heads in the sand, or more likely under the duvet. Others may burn the candle at both ends, never truly acknowledging any of their small wins because they are always holding out for something bigger and better. Please be aware, nothing is ever good enough for the inner critic. This part of us will find fault in absolutely everything.

A small change in response to your inner critic

A small yet effective change you can make is to recognise your inner critic for what she is. When you notice yourself go into an internally critical monologue, stop. Pause, then take three deep, connected in and out breaths.

For example, if your inner critic is telling you that you are lazy, ask yourself if there is any grain of truth in that. There often is at least some grain of truth in these overly critical comments. So, if necessary, choose one small toward move that you can make to address these criticisms, such as sending one email that you have been procrastinating about.

Secondly, and perhaps more importantly, extend some kindness and compassion to yourself. Listening to your inner critic can feel a bit like getting a really bad work review. Extend the same kindness to yourself as you would to someone else if they had been listening to the tirade of criticism you've just endured.

THE COMPARE BEAR

This part of you is constantly comparing yourself to others. The compare bear is obsessed with evaluating whether you are better or worse than others across a broad range of domains – ability, talent, attractiveness, and success. For the most part you come out with the short end of the stick. The compare bear will say, 'why can't you have a great job like so-and-so?' or 'why can't your relationship be as happy as that couple's?' or 'you are not as pretty as her, so why would anyone want you first?' Sometimes your compare bear will compare you favourably to others, but this can put you in a constant state of high alert as you try to live up to those comparisons.

A small change in response to your compare bear

As best you can, slow down your breathing. Now, imagine that you are acknowledging these comparisons, as if you were reading them in a cheesy tabloid or on a news site that you have little respect for. This should help you to see them for what they are – a string of comparisons that may or may not be based on reality.

As with responding to your inner critic, acknowledge if these comparisons are highlighting an area of your life that you want to change. If so, find one small toward move that you can engage in to bring you closer to this reality. However, if you notice the comparison is only because you think you *should* be different rather than its being linked to your values, simply acknowledge it as ungrounded and ultimately unimportant to you.

THE OVERPROTECTIVE PARENT

If you have children, you know that the desire to protect them is paramount. Similarly, if you had a fairly secure childhood, you understand that your parents felt the same way about you. We internalise this parent, who is constantly looking out for any possible risks. When your mind becomes the overprotective parent, it may seem like you are in a state of red alert – you will constantly see dangers and go into survival mode. For example, your internalised overprotective parent will generally urge you away from taking risks, such as starting a new relationship or applying for a new job, because it wants to minimise the chances of you being disappointed.

A small change in response to your overprotective parent

We love to think that our overprotective parent is being irrational all of the time. Sometimes, this is the case, but other times, there is an element of truth in its concerns.

Imagine looking at the situation that your overprotective parent is cautioning you about from the perspective of someone you trust. Now follow through on whatever guidance this trusted ally would give you.

Your overprotective parent truly aims to have your best interests at heart, but is generally motivated more by fear, and therefore by away motivation, than by thriving and toward motivation. You can appreciate, therefore, that the underlying intention is solid, yet often misguided.

THE KNOW-IT-ALL

This internal character rewards you with a hit of feel-good when you get something right, and loves to say, 'I told you so', when you get it wrong. This part of you can be somewhat addictive, because when it rewards you, a pleasurable chemical called dopamine is released in the brain. The know-it-all within you is constantly on the lookout for patterns, and to confirm all of its theories and hypotheses. It says things like, 'I knew that relationship wouldn't work out', or 'I could have told you that you shouldn't have gone out drinking after work.'

A small change in response to your know-it-all

As genuinely as possible, thank your inner know-it-all for his perceptive skills. Then ask him if he has any guidance for you right now. If we befriend our inner know-it-all, he can become an ally rather than a bully.

THE ENTHUSIAST

This part of you just loves the thrill of doing something new and gets overly excited by all the possibilities. When your inner enthusiast is at the front of your mind, you will feel like you are boundless and limitless. Your enthusiast says things like, 'Sure, I can do that task by tomorrow', when in reality it would take a lot longer than that. Or, 'Of course I can pick up the cake for the birthday party. While I'm in town, would you like me to pick up the balloons, candles, card and present? It would be no problem. A pleasure, even.' When you are overly enthusiastic, you may say yes to way more than is actually possible for you to do. This is where the small things add up and very quickly become overwhelming.

A small change in response to your enthusiast

If you can recognise yourself in this description, you may need to practise curbing your enthusiasm. When you are asked to do something, take a couple of breaths. Rather than automatically letting your inner enthusiast become external, take a moment to choose an action guided by your values, what you really want out of life. Make a choice that is right for you, accordingly.

If you grew up in an environment where it was highly prized to please others, and to treat their needs as more important than yours, it may be particularly challenging for you to curb your enthusiasm. It may be massively outside of your comfort zone to say no when you know that this will let someone down or is likely to illicit an unwanted internal response within the other person, such as sadness, resentment, disappointment or anger. You may need to practise a number of small skills to help maintain your motivation. We will cover many such skills in Part Three, 'The Power of Small Toolkit'.

For now, it's important to remember that you might not even know what you truly want yourself, outside of helping and pleasing others, if this has been a very strong influencing factor in your life thus far. Through experimenting with the various small skills within this book, your core inner values will become clearer over time. Sometimes, they will only become obvious based on your feelings after the fact. For example, if you notice that you frequently feel resentful or burned out, you may need to experiment with curbing your enthusiasm, even though there isn't yet a clear underlying value guiding this small change.

TODAY'S SMALL STEP

Your internalised characters

In your small steps diary, take some time to recognise and reflect on which internalised characters you carry around with you. Choose one to look at in more detail. What does he or she sound like in your head? And how do they affect your actions? Be as honest and compassionate with yourself as possible. For the next two days, practise the small change outlined in this chapter for each of your internalised characters.

16
What's Your Story?

Most people prefer the certainty of misery to the misery of uncertainty. Virginia Satir

Our rational mind just loves it when things get nicely wrapped up in a convenient package. Our brains get a good hit of dopamine – that feel-good chemical – anytime we're able to categorise, predict or label an experience into a rational, coherent narrative.

However, incoherent events occur in our lives all the time, and that's hard for our logical mind to accept. If something unwanted happens to us, such as losing a job, a loved one dying, or a relationship breaking down, we may find ourselves asking the question, 'Why did this happen?' or 'What did I do to deserve this?' We also might find ourselves saying things like, 'This just doesn't make any sense.'

Left unchecked in this situation, our inner compare bear

will go into complete overdrive, reeling back over all our past experiences and all the pieces of information we've built up in our framework, either through direct experience, what we know of other people's experiences, or what we have seen in the media. The goal of our inner compare bear is to try and fit everything into a rational narrative so that we can make sense of our pain.

Fake news

Thoughts are not facts, yet our minds incessantly generate 'fake news', accepting thought as fact in an attempt to keep fear at bay. There are few things more fearful than failure and rejection. This goes back to our hunter-gatherer roots – we need to succeed and be part of a group in order to survive. So, our inner brain is incredibly sensitive to even the smallest and most subtle signs of potential rejection.

Let's say an issue arises between you and a friend. Your mind sifts through all its internal data to find incidents in the past that are relevant to your current situation. Depending on your life history and how you've internalised experiences, you may blame yourself or your friend for what's going on. Your mind combines all of your past experiences to generate an edict such as 'It must be me, I'm the problem', or 'People can't be trusted, they always let you down in the end.' We jump between blaming ourselves or others in different circumstances, based on our past lived experiences.

These edicts produce a temporary feeling of safety in the known, rather than danger in the unknown. It's as though you have cracked the code, and now stand a better chance if a similar event happens in future. But all too often, what actually happens next is that you get caught up in one of the four thinking traps we discussed earlier: the pink elephant trap (as you try and suppress your thoughts, they become bigger), the blinkered trap (your overview of the situation becomes blinkered by your thoughts), the washing machine trap (all your thoughts are on a constant spin cycle) or the deep-end trap, attempting to unblinker uncomfortable thoughts that are outside your self-care zone. There's also a fifth trap, however; one your mind often falls into when something challenging happens.

The coherency trap

The coherency trap is particularly dangerous because it uses logic and rationale to lure you in. It seems like such a helpful ally, and sometimes it can be. But, caught in the coherency trap, you can end up jumping to incorrect, and perhaps even unhelpful, conclusions.

Sally's narrative

Sally came to see us because she desperately wanted to be in a committed, loving, intimate relationship. In her early 40s, she was a successful lawyer on a six-figure income. Her coherency trap — when things didn't go right with the guys she was dating — was to buy into the belief that all men are insecure, and that their masculinity is threatened by strong, successful women.

Sally was in a long term relationship in her late 20s, just as her career was taking off. As she became more successful, her boyfriend became more distant, and bit by bit a framework built up so that she began to equate her success with abandonment. When the relationship eventually ended, it provided proof that her coherent narrative about male insecurity was true: that, put off by her success, every man would abandon her. Since then she has dated other men who seemed put off by her strong opinions and earning power, too, and this has fed into her coherent narrative. Believing this narrative, Sally can avoid looking at any of her own away moves in relation to men.

One of Sally's away moves when dating guys was to hide even the slightest hint of vulnerability or imperfection about herself. One of her tactics was to talk a lot about her success, to recount her achievements and name-drop the high-profile people that she knows. We looked at the motivations underlying these away moves for Sally.

Beneath all her talk, Sally was deeply afraid of not being enough. Apart from the coherent narrative she'd built up about male insecurity and abandonment, she had learned in her career that if you wanted to succeed like the big guys, you had to act like the big guys, and part of that was exhibiting a bravado to keep you in the running.

Sally's 5-minute breakout

Sally's 5-minute breakout involved some small shifts that she could make so that she could still present as a strong, successful woman, yet make space for her vulnerabilities too. She was well within her comfort zone when discussing high-profile cases and the sphere in which she moved, but she shied away from talking about other important aspects of herself, around which she was more insecure.

Through our work with her, we'd discovered that Sally had creative writing ambitions, specifically to write a novel. She had gone so far as to write the beginnings of a few chapters, but this was something she'd told no one else about. Also, we realised that Sally was inconsistent in her willingness to write, only doing so on holidays and extended time off work, as she wanted to write perfectly.

Sally's initial 5-minute breakout for herself was to spend at least five minutes each evening writing for her novel after work. This was a challenge for Sally as she often got blinkered by the thoughts, 'What's the point in writing for just five minutes?' and 'I'm too exhausted to write anything worth writing after a long day at work.' Some days Sally only wrote for the five minutes, particularly if she was really tired. She was surprised to find that dedicating a little time each day really helped her to keep her novel in mind daily. Other days, she thought she was very tired yet found that writing gave her energy, and she kept writing for 30 minutes.

Sally's second 5-minute breakout involved dating. We asked her to open up to the guy she was currently dating about her love of writing and her own efforts at it, if only for five minutes. This was a move outside her strong, successful comfort zone because Sally worried that her writing was no good, and that she would not have success as a novelist. It was a small toward move, because she only had to talk about it. She didn't have to show him her work or commit to a deadline.

Sally was surprised at the change in the atmosphere when she opened up about her creative ambitions. Her date was interested to hear more and asked her lots of questions, and she found herself thoroughly enjoying the evening.

Another toward move for Sally was to suggest doing something together with her date that she wasn't expert at, like bowling or skating. These moves were the beginning of Sally breaking free of her coherency trap. In small ways, five minutes at a time, she didn't have to appear always perfect and successful, and in finding some equal ground she could relax her narrative about men all being insecure. Sally didn't stay dating the same man, but she's now happily in a relationship with someone else.

TODAY'S SMALL STEP

What's your story?

Are there any (in)coherent narratives you've built up internally over the years? Here's a three-step way of identifying one.

1. Think of a story that you have about yourself, that connects you to an area of your life you're unhappy

with. Write down as much as you can about why you believe this is so.

2. Now do your best to write down other facets that are also true about your life, which could be the reason why this area of your life is the way that it is.

3. Spot the incoherency, and acknowledge that there may be another way to view your life.

Now identify one small toward move that you could make to break free of that particular coherency trap, and write it down in your small steps diary.

Part Three

The Power of
Small Toolkit

17
Slow and Steady Wins the Race

*Most of the shadows of this life are caused by standing
in one's own sunshine.*
Ralph Waldo Emerson

In this part of the book we will provide you with a toolkit of skills and exercises to bring the Power of Small fully into your daily life. From here on in, you will be changing your actions, one small step at a time, so that you can take your power back, little by little, in consistent and sustainable ways. You will learn how to shift from big problems, to manageable and meaningful solutions.

We will also teach you a number of simple toward moves that will form the basis of small changes that make the difference between a life half-lived and the life you've always dreamed of.

But first, a little story . . . .

The white tiger's cage

In the 1960s, President Dwight D Eisenhower received, on behalf of the American people, the gift of a rare and beautiful white tiger named Mohini. The magnificent Mohini was sent to live at the Washington DC zoo and, as was the norm at the time, was housed in a 12 x 12 foot cage. For years this beautiful creature paced her cage, walking continuously in the same figure of eight pattern hundreds of times a day.

A wealthy benefactor eventually took pity on Mohini, and a new lush, sprawling habitat was created so the tiger could run, stretch, climb and explore. Her new home included several acres of trees, grassy hills and a pond. This new home resembled far more closely the natural surroundings she was born into in her native India.

However, when Mohini arrived at her new, lush home, she didn't react the way everyone expected. She didn't rush out, eagerly exploring and adopting what seemed to be her natural habitat. Instead, she immediately ran to a far corner by the wall, marked off a 12 x 12 foot square for herself, and stayed in that square pacing until the area was worn bare. By the time the physical bars impeding her were removed, Mohini was convinced her 'place' was just a 12 x 12 foot square. Everything in her physiology told her that she must stay in her self-imposed cage, and she stayed within it until she was put down at the age of 20, crippled with arthritis.

Mohini's story demonstrates the classic conditioning most of us live by when we become stuck in self-limiting stories, hemmed in by the rules that block us from stepping out of our comfort zones. Mohini was a magnificent, powerful creature who lived in an invisible cage, as if her survival depended on it.

You too are a magnificent, powerful creature. But the difference is, you can keep talking small steps beyond the invisible cage you've confined yourself to until this invisible cage no longer dictates your actions and inactions.

Slow and steady wins the race

This life you wish you were living is not for some future, ideal version of you to enjoy when you've proven yourself worthy or feel deserving of it. You already have everything you need right inside of you to live a life that will lead to more satisfaction and fulfilment, without the need to reach big achievements or lofty goals. By all means you can have big achievements and set lofty goals, but this is not necessary for you to live a life worth fighting for.

The ultimate aim when we are working with anyone using the Power of Small skill set, the construction of a life worth fighting for by taking small, tangible steps each and every day. It's not a transformational 'before and after' process. It takes daily practice, patience and, most of all, commitment.

It's about living your best life today in small ways, rather than planning and working towards the ideal version in your head. If the zoo had expanded Mohini's environment little by little, from 12 x 12 feet to 13 x 13 feet, gradually increasing the size of her environment, slowly but surely she would have adjusted. This is also the case for you.

We want a life for you that is built around a deep motivation based on your own values, rather than being shaped by external rules, social expectations and internalised shoulds and musts.

However, expanding beyond the limits of your comfort zone also means challenging the rules that have kept you stuck, and when you initially start to challenge those rules, your internalised overprotective parent will fight back.

Slow and steady progress – one small step at a time – will win over, until your overprotective parent is aligned with what is actually best for you.

TODAY'S SMALL STEP

Acknowledge how your life resembles Mohini's

Similar to Mohini, you might be held back by restrictions that are no longer actually in place. Divide a sheet in your small steps diary in two. On the top half, write down the actions you engage in when you are caught in your own version of a 12 x 12 foot invisible cage. Really connect to the unwanted thoughts, emotions and bodily sensations this stirs up in you.

On the bottom half of the page, acknowledge what your version of expansive would be. Give yourself a chance to fully connect to the thoughts, emotions and bodily sensations that this brings up as you break out of your invisible cage.

Decide on one action that is small and manageable enough for you to engage in right now that will be one step in that direction, for example, signing up for a class or reaching out to an old friend.

18

Choose One Area of Your Life to Work On

Trying to do it all, be it all and have it all is exhausting. All too often people find themselves asking, 'What was it all for?' The sad conclusion for so many is that the things they pushed themselves to do and have were rarely that important and never led to the happy and fulfilling life they longed for. Domonique Bertolucci

When working with the Power of Small toolkit, it is helpful to break down the exercise into smaller chunks, by using the toolkit with just one of the four main areas of your life. These four areas centre on relationships, life purpose and contribution, health and wellbeing, and fun and downtime.

If you are overwhelmed in more than one area of your life, you may not be sure where to begin. In this chapter we will repeat a similar process for each of the four main areas, so you can establish a good idea of which one you want to start working on and how to proceed after that. You can come back to this chapter at any time if you want to apply the Power of Small toolkit to another area of your life.

It is important to write your answers in your small steps diary. Don't sweat it too much; just jot down what comes to mind.

Relationships

The quality of your relationships plays a crucial and critical role in your overall quality of life, health and wellbeing. It's important to check in regularly to figure out if your small actions within relationships are guided by your deepest values, or are merely a manifestation of your unwanted emotions.

Seven questions to ask yourself about relationships

When you read the words 'key relationships' in these questions, it's best for the moment to consider maybe just one or two key relationships in your life. You can always come back and answer those questions again in relation to any other relationships you have.

1. In an ideal world, if you were absolutely grounded in your values, how would you like to see yourself responding in relationships? Be as specific as you can, acknowledging what this would look like from the outside looking in, and what it would feel like from the inside out.

2. Are there, or have there been, any challenging relationships in your life? (Most of us have had at least some.) Is there a clear pattern that you can identify in these relationships in terms of how you respond/responded?

3. On a scale of one to ten, how satisfied are you with the key relationships in your life? Examples of key relationships include intimate relationships, parent-child, sibling, friend, or work-related relationships.

4. In your key relationships, on a scale of one to ten, how much do you believe you are responding in ways that are guided by your values? One indicates that your values are not apparent in the slightest; ten indicates that even when relationships are difficult, you can rest assured that you are responding entirely in line with your values.

5. What difference would it make to your overall quality of life if you continued to respond in the way that you have been in your key relationships? As best you can, connect with the immediate, short-, medium-, and long term consequences of this.

6. What difference would it make to your overall quality of life if you changed how you respond in your key relationships? As best you can, connect

with the immediate, short-, medium-, and long term impacts of this.

7. On a scale of one to ten, how important is it to look at this area first, before looking at the other three main areas of your life?

Purpose and contribution

We all need to feel like we have purpose in life, and that our actions are contributing to something other than ourselves. Purpose and contribution can include paid employment and formal study. However, it can also include voluntary work, work within the home or family unit informal learning through online courses, and activities such as writing or other creative pursuits.

Seven questions to ask yourself about purpose and contribution

1. What gives you a sense of purpose and contribution? If you can't think of something recent, travel back to a moment when you felt a great sense of satisfaction in what you were doing.

2. Who do you admire in terms of purpose and contribution? Sometimes, it's difficult to connect to this aspect of ourselves, so it can be useful to connect to potential role models who might help you gain some clarity around what matters to you.

3. On a scale of one to ten, how satisfied are you
    with your sense of life purpose and levels of
    contribution right now? One indicates that you
    feel completely devoid of purpose, meaning and a
    sense of contribution; ten indicates that you feel
    completely aligned with your sense of purpose and
    contribution.

4. In the area of purpose and contribution, on a scale
    of one to ten, how much do you believe your values
    guide your actions and inactions? One indicates
    that your values are not obvious or apparent in
    the slightest; ten indicates that you are responding
    entirely in line with your values. (Please note that
    we get very few tens in the areas of purpose and
    contribution. Most of us have unlived dreams of
    what we would really love to do in our lives, yet we
    listen to our internal overprotective parent who is
    on constant damage limitation.)

5. What difference would it make to your overall
    quality of life if you continued to respond in
    the way that you have been in terms of purpose
    and contribution? As best you can, connect with
    the immediate, short-, medium-, and long term
    consequences of this.

6. What difference would it make to your overall
    quality of life if you changed how you respond in

terms of purpose and contribution? As best you can, connect with the immediate, short-, medium-, and long term impacts of this.

7. On a scale of one to ten, how important is it to look at this area first, before looking at the other three main areas of your life?

Health and wellbeing

There's a lot of truth in the saying, 'your health is your wealth'. If you've ever been unwell either physically or psychologically, you have seen how your perception of yourself, others and the world around you is greatly affected by your health, or lack thereof. Our physical health and psychological wellbeing filter all other aspects of our lives.

Seven questions to ask yourself about health and wellbeing

1. What does ideal physical health and psychological wellbeing mean to you? To help answer this, consider how you would recognise it if you saw it in yourself or others.

2. If you were watching a video of yourself acting in ways that made the most of your physical and psychological health, what would this look like? (Many of us have a picture of ideal health and wellbeing that might not be possible or available to

us through no fault of our own, so it is important to be somewhat realistic given our current life circumstances.) Be as practical and tangible as possible.

3. On a scale of one to ten, how satisfied are you with your health and wellbeing right now? One indicates that you feel completely unhealthy in both body and mind; ten indicates that you feel on top of the world, with no further adjustments or improvements needed.

4. In the area of health and wellbeing, on a scale of one to ten, how much do you believe your actions and inactions are guided by your values? One indicates that your values are not obvious or apparent in the slightest in terms of your actions; ten indicates that you are responding entirely in line with your values. (Please note that we get very few tens in the area of health and wellbeing also. Most of us have at least some, if not many, actions that sabotage our ideal health and wellbeing.)

5. What difference would it make to your overall quality of life if you continued to respond in the way that you have been in terms of your physical health and psychological wellbeing? As best you can, connect with the immediate, short-, medium-, and long term consequences of this.

6. What difference would it make to your overall quality of life if you changed how you respond in terms of your physical health and psychological wellbeing? As best you can, connect with the immediate, short-, medium-, and long term impacts of this.

7. On a scale of one to ten, how important is it to look at this area first, before looking at the other three main areas of your life?

Fun and downtime

Interestingly, this is the one that most of the people we work with skip over, dismissing the impact that fun and downtime have on all the other parts of their lives. It's an area that is very often perceived as a luxury, rather than at best a necessity, and at worst, downright self-indulgent. However, our ability to have fun and get some downtime has a surprisingly large impact on the other three areas we've looked at.

Seven questions to ask yourself about fun and downtime

1. Do you notice a resistance to even looking at the area of fun and downtime in the first place? As best you can, recognise all your judgements, evaluations and comparisons about this area of your life.

2. What does fun and downtime look like for you? If you've got completely bogged down in work, family or health issues, please know that you are not alone. Even if you need to go back months, years or decades, connect to at least three activities in the past that you've found fun and which gave you a sense of refreshment.

3. On a scale of one to ten, how satisfied are you with your levels of fun and downtime right now? One indicates that you feel completely devoid of fun and downtime; ten indicates that you have the optimal levels of fun and downtime that refresh and nourish you while still keeping you on track in the other areas of your life. (Note: if you spend all day every day watching TV, playing computer games or surfing the internet, this, more often than not, is not truly a ten on fun and downtime, as you are likely mindless rather than mindful when engaging in these activities.)

4. In the area of fun and downtime, on a scale of one to ten, how much do you believe your actions and inactions are guided by your values? One indicates that your values are not obvious or apparent in the slightest in terms of your actions; ten indicates that you are responding entirely in line with your values.

5. What difference would it make to your overall quality of life if you continued to respond in the way that you have been in terms of fun and downtime? As best you can, connect with the immediate, short-, medium-, and long term consequences of this.

6. What difference would it make to your overall quality of life if you changed how you respond in terms of fun and downtime? As best you can, connect with the immediate, short-, medium-, and long term impacts of this.

7. On a scale of one to ten, how important is it to look at this area first, before looking at the other three main areas of your life?

TODAY'S SMALL STEP

Choose one area to start with

It's likely that your ratings are down at the lower end of the scale in more than one of the four areas of your life, and you may now find yourself wanting to change every area of your life all at once.

However, if you cast your net too wide and attempt to make changes in multiple areas simultaneously, you are likely to become so overwhelmed that you'll either burn yourself out, or you won't even get started in the first place. With this in mind, having completed the seven-question check-in in each of the four main areas of your life, choose one area to start with.

Think of these four areas as all being the corners of a rough diamond. Each corner that you carefully polish will often have a knock-on positive impact on at least one of the other corners. For example, often if you work on your personal growth, this will help your relationships also, and vice versa.

As always, choose an area that is outside of your comfort zone, yet firmly planted within your self-care zone.

If you're keen to dive in further, check out some of the skills in the next few chapters to help you make more progress in the area that you have chosen.

19
Living a Life of Minimal Regrets

It is only when we truly know and understand that we have a limited time on earth, and that we have no way of knowing when our time is up, that we will begin to live each day to the fullest, as if it were the only one we had. Elizabeth Kübler Ross

When you're stuck operating from threat mode even when it's not appropriate, life can feel like a constant state of fire-fighting and problem solving. You don't have time to deal with anything but the most urgent issue in front of you, as you function in damage control mode. Sometimes all it takes is one small shift to stop this spin cycle and help you get some space to productively deal with what you can, ahead of time.

Setting conscious small intentions for each day, and letting your values be a guide for acting on a daily basis, are key. Following through on these actions consistently, while being in touch with your truth and what you truly want, means that you can respond from a grounded place when life throws unexpected things your way, rather than waiting to react in the moment.

Our reactions are often overly fuelled by overwhelming emotions, thoughts or images flooding our brains. As such, the actions from a place of reaction are often the very opposite of the actions we would choose if we were operating from our values.

The top five regrets of the dying

Bronnie Ware, an Australian nurse who worked for many years in palliative care, shared the top five regrets of the dying that she heard most often. We'd like to share them with you here.

1. I wish I'd had the courage to live a life true to myself, not the life others expected of me.

2. I wish I didn't work so hard.

3. I wish I'd had the courage to express my feelings.

4. I wish I'd stayed in touch with friends.

5. I wish that I had let myself be happier.

Here's the interesting thing: regret while you are still alive can motivate you to make small changes on a daily basis, which can be a very helpful thing. According to psychologist

Neal Roese's research, regret was rated most powerful in a list of 'negative' emotions that help us to:

1. Make sense of the world

2. Avoid future unhelpful behaviours

3. Gain insight

4. Achieve social harmony

5. Improve our ability to approach desired opportunities

Five ways to prevent regret

Many people live their lives running from one thing to the next without any real grounding or connection to what matters. This is essentially how we give our power away in multiple small ways each and every day, which leads to us living a half-lived life, if even that. The Power of Small is about shifting our lives in small ways to take that power back. Here are five tenets of the process, which are designed so that you will not share the top five regrets of the dying:

1. We consistently encourage you to be more courageous and live a life that is truer to you. Connect with what's important to you on a daily basis and take at least one small step every day outside your comfort zone towards what's most important. This might involve you saying yes to

things that you previously would've said no to for fear of others' judgements, such as dance or acting classes if this is your cup of tea.

2. We ask you to reflect on the intentions underlying the work that you do, rather than blindly working long hours every week simply because you have bought into a belief that you need to do this to be worthy. It's true that most of us need to work in order to earn money. However, we can be more consciously aware of how much money we actually need (truly *need*, as opposed to want), in order to move closer to what really matters; as opposed to our motivation to earn being driven by needs, shoulds and musts to live that bigger, better, faster life.

3. Every time you push your feelings down and brush them under the carpet, this has an impact. We encourage you to express your feelings more in small and consistent ways. We don't mean all of your emotions, all of the time, but in those instances when expressing your emotions is likely to bring you closer to what and who you want to be in life.

4. We ask you to connect to people in meaningful ways. Isolation and lack of contact with friends and loved ones is as detrimental to our health and wellbeing as smoking 15 cigarettes a day or being obese.

5. We encourage you to find the small things that make a big difference in your life. For some of you, this may be taking a short walk. For others, it may be having a brief phone call or meeting with a loved one – or taking ten minutes to concentrate on your own needs rather than those of your children/family. The Power of Small is about identifying these small acts and engaging in them.

A three-step process to foster a life of minimal regrets

1. Once per day, ask yourself the question, 'Is there anything I'm holding back from doing today because I'm worried about what others might think of me?'

2. If the answer is yes, explore this option and ask yourself, 'Would this action bring me closer to my values?'

3. If the answer is yes, see if you'd be willing to take one small step to bring you closer towards engaging in this action.

TODAY'S SMALL STEP

Consider your top five regrets, right now.

This exercise can be a little scary for some people to

engage in, yet it is one that people we work with have found most helpful.

In your small steps diary, write your top five regrets about how you live your life right now. You can have some of the same regrets as the top five regrets of the dying; or they can be totally different.

Once you have acknowledged your top five regrets, find a small action that you can take right now to bring you one step closer to living a life with minimal such regrets going forward.

It's important to note that we do not engage in any action on a long term basis unless there is some gain in this action for us. Very often these actions will help us to avoid unwanted thoughts, emotions or bodily sensations in the short term. We will be addressing exactly what you can do to change your relationship to these unwanted internal experiences in the coming chapters.

20

Let Things Get a Little Messy

Nothing any good isn't hard.
F Scott Fitzgerald

Our mind is almost always trying to problem solve and protect us from harm. It is on near constant damage-control alert, fuelled by our red alert threat system. This part of our being has a strong evolutionary reason for existing. We evolved to survive and in order to survive, we needed to avoid anything that threatened our ability to stay alive or stay within a group. Therefore, our brains have maintained this red alert threat system in an attempt to prevent us from failing or being rejected. However, when we stop to question the usefulness and the validity of our coping strategies, they are often nothing more than knee-jerk threat reactions with little value.

Your unhelpful predictions that you won't land the job you

want, or that you'll perform poorly giving a speech, or that you won't enjoy your date, all serve to keep you protected. They stop you from getting hurt, but the thing is, they also stop you from experiencing any kind of growth.

To fully live in a connected and authentic way means expanding to make room for all that life has to offer. The more you put yourself out there, the more you risk getting knocked back or failing. However, you also drastically increase your chances of living a life worth fighting for.

Small shift in perspective

The only way to maintain balance, stability, and a false sense of predictability in life is to not take a step. If you're unwilling to make room for a certain amount of discomfort in your life, chances are you'll need to stay very still and not make a move at all. If, on the other hand, you are sick and tired of how things are and want to make changes, you need to make room in your life for things to get a little messy.

A rich and meaningful life is not a pain-free life, or one where we don't suffer – that is just a safe life where nothing much tends to happen. If you want more in your life, you need to make room for everything: the good, the bad and the ugly. We cannot selectively numb out those things that we don't want to engage with.

A life worth fighting for is not a comfortable or safe life, and it's definitely not one you can predict or control. It's where you find the small experiences that stack up to build the life you truly long for, that feels authentically yours.

Openness to learn from new experiences and willingness to accept the discomfort of doing new, difficult and unfamiliar things is an essential outlook of a life worth fighting for. You need to develop willingness to make mistakes, openness to messing up and getting it wrong. You can then learn when things don't work out, which sometimes they inevitably won't.

Are you willing to feel uncomfortable, to experience fear, to sit with uncertainty, if doing so moves you closer to what really matters?

Accepting pain

Expanding towards your values means making room for the obstacles and challenges that this inevitably brings. We could all learn a thing or two from improv (improvisational comedy and improvisational theatre), which teaches us to say 'yes and' to new opportunities that come our way. By responding to our lives from a 'yes and' vantage point, we are making the best of the life that we are living rather than some idealised, and unrealistic, version of our lives that we have built up in our heads.

This is counterintuitive to many of us. We are more accustomed to fighting against our life and our experience when it does not measure up to what we wanted or expected. Yet, in denying our reality, we essentially deny our lives and ourselves as they currently are, rendering us powerless to change. The Power of Small approach is not a life minus pain, it's a life expanded, little by little, around the pain. For those interested in learning more about improv, we recommend *The Improviser's Way* by Katy Schutte.

Pain exists as part of life. However, you don't have to live your life in suffering. The Power of Small encourages us all to create a life beyond the suffering we're enduring. When we are not engaging in small actions to expand our lives around our pain, our life can start to feel very small, stale and stagnant. In fact, our life might start to feel like it is all about pain and that there is very little life to be lived outside of this pain. Actions consistently aimed towards minimising pain and discomfort inadvertently minimise the size and quality of our lives.

You can't get rid of the pain, but you can have so much more in your life. And yes, you risk more pain and vulnerability by expanding your life beyond your comfort zone, but you will also have so much more amazing, life-enhancing and exciting experiences.

You may not be able to control, get rid of, or manage your difficult life experiences, or your challenging emotions like anxiety or sadness, but they no longer have to hold you back. Each step that you take beyond what your mind considers possible for you is challenging the validity of the claim that pain should be avoided at all costs. And the more small steps you take towards the experiences that you want to define your life, the more such steps will become your guiding force.

TODAY'S SMALL STEP

Engage in active acceptance

As best you can, see if you can allow an unwanted feeling, such as overwhelm, to be there. You don't have to like it or want it – simply allow it to be as it is physically in your body, rather than getting overly consumed by what your mind tells you this feeling means.

It's really important here to make the distinction between passive resignation (or grudging tolerance), and an actual allowing or acceptance of your unwanted emotions. If you are doing this exercise while saying something like, 'I guess I'll just have to accept this emotion, then' with disdain or numbness and more than a hint of resentment, chances are you're engaging in passive resignation rather than active acceptance.

The act of passive resignation is not helpful for our health and wellbeing, and it is, in fact, disempowering. The act of active acceptance, on the other hand, is incredibly empowering. If in doubt, check in to notice if you feel more empowered or disempowered by the act of allowing. Give it time – take five minutes for this exercise and don't judge the processes that happen during that time. Check in with how you feel at the end. Has anything shifted? If it has, then you have sat with discomfort actively. Practise this exercise on a daily basis, and notice what begins to happen between you and your relationship with uncomfortable emotions. Like any exercise, the more we flex the muscle, the more adept we become at it.

21

Tuning in to Your Five Senses

*We will be more successful in all our endeavours if we can let go
of the habit of running all the time and take little pauses to relax
and re-centre ourselves. And we'll also have a lot more
joy in living.* Thich Nhat Hanh

Sometimes in life, major issues will hit you unexpectedly, or
arise as a result of something entirely outside your control.
Other than respond as best you can in the moment when they
happen, there isn't a whole lot you can really do to prepare.

Aside from these major events, however, there are
numerous tiny things you do every single day that have
the potential to either help you or trip you up. How you
choose to respond or react depends on how connected and
present you are in your own life, in your relationships, and
in yourself. By practising some small skills on a daily basis,
you will respond far better to the unwanted small stuff that

inevitably arises, as well as the major unwanted life events that we all experience.

Living on autopilot

Perhaps you take the same route to and from work every day. It becomes such a familiar route that most times you don't consciously think about the turns and actions you take to get to your destination. You might even notice that you're home with your key in the door before you realise it. You may even move house or change job, and one day end up back at your old house or workplace, because your mind has been elsewhere. This is a type of automatic thinking and living, and for the most part, it serves us very well.

We are bombarded with so many stimuli and messages on a daily basis that we've needed to develop a filtering system, so that our brains can concentrate on the really important information processing. However, when we find ourselves stuck in a place whereby our lives feel like movie images on a distant screen, or that we're sleepwalking through our days, we need to step out of our heads and plug fully into life through all our senses.

Some examples of autopilot living

Kate is preoccupied with her internalised feelings of overwhelm due to the amount she has on her plate, as she attempts to balance her home and work lives. When she is in work, she is frequently thinking about her two young children and feeling guilty that she's not spending time with them. When she goes on autopilot, her small away moves involve half-reading her emails and responding to what she thinks are the salient parts. She frequently misses important pieces of information, and as such, has made the wrong call or not acknowledged and responded appropriately to an important email from her line manager.

Similarly, when she's at home, Kate is frequently thinking about all that she has to do at work and how far behind she is. Her small autopilot away move here involves checking her work emails on her smartphone while she's feeding the children or doing their homework with them. Her children often have to say the same thing to her three or four times before it fully registers with her.

Ben is completely overwhelmed by the process of setting up his business. He is frequently in his car going from meeting to meeting, trying to secure as many funders and supporters as possible in an attempt to ensure that his start-up won't fail.

In his car, Ben's small away move is rehearsing the conversations he wants to have with potential investors to the point where he is driving on autopilot, not fully aware of his surroundings.

Julie has decided that this will be the year she will meet someone and have a meaningful relationship, so she's dating a lot of guys via Tinder.

Her small away move is going into complete autopilot mode on these dates, running a checklist of what she wants her date to be like, from height and interests to income earned, and also a checklist of what she wants to convey about herself to her date. As a result, these encounters start to feel like a job interview, which, let's face it, isn't very romantic. She gets little or no enjoyment out of them and they frequently don't lead to anything.

Mental experiencing

Autopilot mode is where we are most likely to use unhelpful default strategies for coping, without even knowing we are doing it until it's too late. Autopilot mode involves being fully immersed in our mental experiences. If you're unsure of what we mean, think of those moments where you are eating, yet not tasting your food, or you are in a conversation yet not really hearing what the other person is saying.

Of course, we all need to go into our mental experiences from time to time. This allows us to make sense of what's going on in the world. But if we check in with our mental experiences and return to our five senses – what we can see, hear, smell, taste and feel in the world – we are likely to make toward moves connected to our values. All too often, though, we stay in our mental experiences, on autopilot mode repeating the same small actions that lead to a half-lived life.

By increasing your awareness of events as they happen in your world, you can recognise when you are acting from unhelpful patterns of behaviour and pivot to a more helpful toward move. There are a variety of small mindfulness-based skills that will help you stay more fully connected to your five senses. From this mode, you can really taste what you're eating and really hear people when you are having a conversation with them. Through learning these small skills, you can make massive improvements to your quality of life.

The power of mindfulness

A core part of the work we do with our clients is teaching them mindfulness-based skills to help increase their ability to respond to life events in ways that are helpful rather than destructive.

Research indicates that mindfulness can be extremely helpful for people who are feeling overwhelmed by the multiple demands in their lives. Mindfulness can help us to develop and maintain more meaningful relationships with others and indeed ourselves, decrease our chances of burnout, increase our productivity and our overall health and wellbeing, while also decreasing our chances of relapsing into depression if we've experienced depression in the past.

Mindfulness-based skills involve you really connecting with your five senses, rather than getting lost in mental experiencing. They involve paying attention in the present moment in a deliberate, conscious, non-judgemental manner.

Rather than getting lost in your mind commentary about an experience, be it a conversation, or a work or family situation, mindfulness-based skills help you to decipher your responses and reactions to this experience in the present moment. In this way, you can learn to respond with small, conscious toward moves rather than reacting automatically, which often involves away moves.

Everyday mindfulness techniques

An important component of mindfulness is creating a time and space in your life to dedicate to formal mindfulness practice in a quiet place where you're unlikely to be disturbed. Having said that, if you are operating at the level where you're already feeling overwhelmed, with little time to complete the basic daily tasks, it's unlikely that you can invest a lot of extra time in formal mindfulness.

With this in mind, the Power of Small mindfulness practices are intended to be very short, and workable. They can be gently and gradually introduced to your day with minimum disruption. You can access audio guides to these practices on our website, and there are also five of our favourite practices in Chapter 30, 'Short Active Reflections'.

From a practical standpoint, it also makes sense that mindfulness skills prove useful when you need them, no matter where you are or what you're doing. So, in addition to the more formal Power of Small mindfulness exercises, we focus on mindfulness skills that you can engage in when you are out and about, living your daily life. These look at how you can transform any small moment from autopilot to five senses experiencing.

Five small everyday mindfulness skills you can apply today

1. In a conversation, notice your mind's tendency to jump forward in time and plan ahead. Deliberately come back to mindfully listening to what the other person is saying to you. Notice the words they are using, their tone of voice and their facial expression. When it is your turn to speak, notice what you genuinely feel, and speak in a way that is guided by this rather than in a non-conscious automatic way.

2. When you are eating, take a moment to notice the food before you put it into your mouth. Simply notice, in as much detail as possible, the qualities and textures, as if it were the first time you've ever seen this particular food.

   Once you start eating, pay attention to what the food tastes and feels like. If you can, slow down your natural rate of eating just a tad and see if this makes any difference to your experience of eating. Consciously tune in to your body to notice when you become full and stop eating before you become overly full.

3. When you are outside, deliberately tune in to your senses of seeing, hearing and feeling. Notice five

things you can see – paying vivid attention to colour, texture and shape. Notice four things you can hear, such as traffic, birds or a distant hum. Notice three things you can feel, such as the air against your skin, some tension or strain in your body, or the feeling of your clothes against your skin.

4. On a usual route that you take, such as to or from work, either via car, public transport or on foot, consciously decide to take this route without headphones or making calls, then deliberately tune in to your five senses and aim to notice three things that you haven't noticed before.

5. Listen to a piece of music. Close your eyes and pay attention only to the music. Notice what you feel as you listen. Notice what thoughts arise within you, yet keep coming back to the music. Notice the sounds and the space between sounds. Notice if this experience is different to when this music is in the background as you go about your daily life.

TODAY'S SMALL STEP

Practice two of the everyday mindfulness skills

Identify which one of the everyday mindfulness skills you

feel most drawn to, and also the one you feel the most resistance to.

Commit to doing these everyday mindfulness skills once a day for a week – even the one you resist. Often the small skills we have most resistance to can be the ones we most need.

Make a note in your small steps diary of what you notice.

22
The Art of Unblinkering

We can spend our whole lives escaping from the monsters of our minds. Pema Chödrön

Many of us spend inordinate amounts of time attempting to escape the monsters of our minds. Our minds have a 24/7 commentary on pretty much every single thing that we do, continually generating a variety of judgements, evaluations and (most often) unhelpful comparisons. The great news is that we can build psychological strength and muscle mass in terms of how we respond to those unwanted and limiting thoughts.

Just like you can become more physically flexible by going to the gym, so too can you become more psychologically flexible by changing how you respond to your unwanted thoughts. We call this skill 'unblinkering'. A really valuable thing about unblinkering is that it can work with thoughts regardless of whether they are right or wrong, true or false, 'good' or 'bad'.

True or false?

The thoughts that can wear us down the most are the ones that are actually true. When we give workshops, we often ask how many people in the room have ever let down people they know and love. About 90 per cent of hands go up. The other 10 per cent are either saints or, more likely, lying.

It is inevitable that we will let down the people we love at certain times in our lives. We can become blinkered by thoughts, judgements and stories about what that means about us as people, and for our relationships.

When we become blinkered by a thought that we have let down someone we love, our red alert system gets activated and we go into damage-control mode. The emotion most likely to show up is shame, and this can prompt us to engage in actions that bring us further away from resolution with our loved one. We make small away moves like avoiding the person, justifying what we did to ourselves or the other person, or trying to downplay or distract from what we've done. These away moves may work for us in the short term, but in the long term they build up to become ultimately harmful to our relationships.

There are also some thoughts that we have about ourselves, such as 'I'm lazy', 'I always quit things', or 'I'm not attractive enough.' Most of us can come up with evidence to support why any one of these thoughts are true. We are all lazy sometimes, and we all have at least some tendency towards procrastination. Similarly, we have all quit some things. This is part of human nature. And unfortunately, pretty much everyone has got some unwanted feedback about their attractiveness at some point or another.

To go around blinkered by those types of thoughts will invariably result in you making many small away moves such as not asserting your needs, and frequently choosing resentment over the discomfort of meeting your own needs. You will most likely fail again and again because you are so blinkered by these limiting thoughts that you are not able to see the opportunities to succeed that present themselves to you on a daily basis.

What's great about unblinkering is that you don't have to attempt to discredit these thoughts and get into an argument about whether they are true or not. The only measure of whether it's beneficial to do thought unblinkering is to ask yourself if you engage in toward or away moves when you are blinkered by a particular thought. If you engage in away moves, then you will benefit from unblinkering.

Good or bad?

Many self-help books try to sell the notion that we need to think positively or have happy thoughts all the time. Alas, this idea is based neither on science nor research.

A large study found that positive affirmations can indeed be helpful if we are already feeling good about ourselves. However, if we are already feeling completely overwhelmed, positive affirmations may do us more harm than good. Also, it can become problematic if we are blinkered by a thought that many would deem to be good or positive. Let's say you are blinkered by the thought that you are absolutely wonderful and that your wants and desires are absolutely paramount.

The away moves you might engage in when blinkered by the thought that 'I'm wonderful and in the right' may include not taking responsibility for your own actions, or you may blame others when things don't work out, thereby not getting to the truth of a matter, and ultimately not growing as a person.

It is best to unblinker from thoughts, even when they feel positive or comforting, if those thoughts lead to you engaging in the same small away moves again and again, which stifle your growth.

Small unblinkering strategies

There isn't a one-size-fits-all unblinkering strategy that works for everyone. Yet anyone who has fully committed to this process has found at least one that works for them. It's important to be really clear in terms of the purpose, 'the why', which underlies unblinkering strategies. The why should never be about getting rid of or minimising the thought itself, or the emotional impact that the thought has on you.

These strategies are designed to help you unblinker from these thoughts so that you can consciously choose to respond to a thought from your core inner values by engaging in a conscious toward move, rather than an automatic away move. In this way, you move from being a passive passenger in your life to taking the driver's seat, steering the course of your life in a clear direction towards what is most important to you.

The measure of success is always determined by whether you engage in a small toward move once you have unblinkered.

You need to be aware of the pink elephant trap when you practise these small strategies. If you apply these strategies with the aim of getting rid of the unwanted thought, you will most likely end up thinking it more rather than less.

It's also best to be cautious of another trap – the deep-end trap. This involves applying these strategies to your most painful, unwanted and limiting thoughts at the beginning. Yes, if you practise unblinkering in an open and consistent manner, you'll be able to use these strategies with even the most unwanted thoughts over time, for instance thoughts linked to great trauma or tragedy in your life. However, just like you needed to learn to swim in the shallow end of the pool before you could venture towards the deep end, so too is the case with unblinkering.

As best you can, apply the following strategies to a thought, or set of thoughts, that is outside of your comfort zone, yet well within your self-care zone. In this way your comfort zone will expand, little by little, so that you may apply these small strategies to even the biggest thoughts.

1. Give yourself permission to indulge yourself (temporarily)

Our seven-step process to writing your uncensored and potentially self-indulgent account of an unwanted situation:

1. Grab a pen and paper or open up a fresh document on your computer.

2. Take a few moments to pause in silence, reflecting on your uncensored, unfiltered thoughts about this situation.

3. Write down as many of these thoughts as possible.

4. Make sure you include judgements, evaluations and any unhelpful comparisons that you have about yourself, others and the situation.

5. Tune in to your inner teenager and write down how they feel about this situation.

6. Listen to the most insecure parts of yourself, which personalise whatever is going on, and write down these thoughts also.

7. Give yourself the freedom to write the thoughts that you would never say in public.

You know you're doing this exercise properly if the thought of anyone reading it makes you want the ground to open and swallow you. What you write here does not have to be politically correct. In fact, it is often petty and petulant, giving you space to externalise even your most whimsical or whiny thoughts.

Sometimes people resist writing these thoughts because they don't want to be self-indulgent. In writing these unfiltered and uncensored thoughts down, you can free yourself to see them for what they are – a commentary on what's going on in your life, rather than your life as it is. As such, it can be tremendously helpful in your quest to unblinker yourself from your unwanted and limiting thoughts. The irony is that by indulging ourselves, and our unwanted thoughts, in small, temporary ways, we can often return to our regular daily life more quickly and effectively.

Sue

Sue was really struggling with her 75-year-old mother's recent diagnosis of dementia. Understandably, she was having a whole host of thoughts, ranging from concern for her mother, to worrying about the impact this would have on the time she could spend with her two teenage children, to berating herself for having such thoughts. When someone is struggling with a loved one's recent diagnosis or health concern, either physical or psychological, it is totally natural to have a whole host of thoughts around the situation. However, modern society often doesn't allow us to acknowledge the full range of our thoughts, especially the ones that we judge as bad, wrong or immoral.

When Sue was asked to engage in this writing your

uncensored thoughts exercise, she was reluctant, to say the least. She protested, 'What good will this do?', 'I'll just get really sad and angry and then I won't be any good to anyone', and 'I don't want to share my uncensored thoughts, maybe you'll judge me.' Such protests, blocks and barriers are pretty standard. Sue was encouraged to do the exercise, and was asked to identify any underlying value that would be important enough to her that she would be willing to experience short-term discomfort. There was a big enough value for Sue — her relationship with her mother, and also her relationships with her partner and children, who she had been increasingly snappy with since her mother's diagnosis.

The exercise was tough for Sue. She acknowledged uncensored thoughts that she would usually hide for fear of being judged or being seen as petty, such as:

- 'Why is this happening to me and my family?'
- 'I shouldn't be so selfish.'
- 'How long will this go on for?'
- 'How bad will this get?'
- 'I'd hate to have dementia. What if this happens to me?'
- 'I don't want to see my mother and witness her deteriorating like this.'
- 'I know I shouldn't think this but sometimes I wish that she would have died rather than this. I'm such a horrible person for thinking that.'
- 'I can't cope.'
- 'I miss my mum.'

· 'I'm angry that she isn't here for me. Oh, how selfish
   and childish am I to have that thought?'

As you can imagine, it wasn't easy for Sue to allow herself to
acknowledge and write down her thoughts. The reality is that
most people in a similar scenario will have at least some, if
not all, of the same thoughts. Yet, many people are afraid to
acknowledge these thoughts to themselves or others for fear
of being viewed as immature, petulant, indulgent or selfish.
The unfortunate side-effect of this suppressing of thoughts is
that they don't go away. In fact, without acknowledgement
and some form of expression, they often grow bigger and
bigger, and the struggle to push them down can lead to
people engaging in multiple small away moves that have a
massive adverse impact on their own lives.

After completing this exercise, Sue initially felt anxiety and
shame. However, when she read it back and asked herself,
'Would I judge my friend if they had these thoughts in this
scenario?' she discovered that the answer was a resounding
no. The act of doing this exercise helped Sue see her thoughts
as thoughts, rather than getting overly blinkered by them. She
then made choices about how much time she would spend with
her mother and her family and made sure to allocate time
for some self-care, which she needed now more than ever,
even though her mind told her that she was 'self-indulgent' for
doing so.

Sue's 5-minute breakout

Although the work Sue did involved writing, her 5-minute

breakout was the opposite of getting her feelings out on paper. We invited her to simply sit quietly with her mother for five minutes each time she visited her.

In situations like Sue's, we often try to find ways to flee from our fears, from our grief, but the more we flee, the more we're paradoxically mired in grief and assailed by fear. We asked Sue to be present with her mother, listening if she talked, saying very little, and allowing her sorrow and fear to simply be. It became a comforting and close, unspoken routine for both women, as Sue's mother began to pick up on her daughter's energy, and to feel quietly supported in her own grief and fear.

2. Cross out the judgements

This strategy can be done either as a follow-on from the previous exercise or completed in its own right. It is particularly helpful if you have a lot of thoughts about a situation that is challenging you.

Write down your account of the situation and your mind's interpretation of the situation. Notice how it feels in your body as you write and then read over what you have written. Now cross out all of the judgements.

A judgement is any interpretation that you make about a situation. For example, if you have the thought, 'he must be so disappointed in me because I let him down', you would cross this out unless he actually told you that he was disappointed in you because he felt let down by you, at which point it becomes a fact.

Judgements are also speculations on others' behaviour. Thoughts like 'she was lying to me' would be crossed out unless you know for sure that she was lying. You can keep facts such as 'she went very red when I asked her where she was last Saturday'. However, any unconfirmed interpretations or assumptions should be crossed out.

See what you are left with. Based on what's left uncrossed, take a moment to pause and extend compassion to yourself, and then choose your next course of action. Make sure this choice is rooted in what matters most to you at this moment in time.

Eric

Eric is very driven to succeed in his workplace and he is also highly aware of anything that he perceives as a negative evaluation of his work. He had got caught up in the washing machine trap following events that had transpired at work over the past few days. He was encouraged to write a paragraph or two about what had happened initially. Here is what he wrote:

I've been trying really hard and nobody seems to acknowledge any of the good that I do. What's the point in trying? I spent a long time trying to come up with a good pitch for marketing our new product. When I pitched it at the meeting, there were a couple of comments and then they moved swiftly to someone else's ideas and they spent much longer on their ideas. I bet they all think that I'm useless. I can just tell by the way they treat other people that they think I'm the weakest link. I need to work much harder to get them to pay more attention to my ideas. Maybe I shouldn't even be working in this company, and go somewhere else where they appreciate me more.

Eric was then asked to go back over the paragraph and cross out all the judgements. This is what he was left with:

~~*I've been trying really hard and nobody seems to acknowledge any of the good that I do. What's the point in trying?*~~ *I spent a long time trying to come up with a good pitch for marketing our new product. When I pitched it at the meeting, there were a couple of comments and then they moved swiftly to someone else's ideas and they spent much longer on their ideas.* ~~*I bet they all think that I'm useless. I can just tell by the way they treat other people that they think I'm the weakest link. I need to work much harder to get them to pay more attention to my ideas. Maybe I shouldn't even be working in this company, and go somewhere else where they appreciate me more.*~~

Can you see the difference between the first and the second paragraph? This was incredibly helpful for Eric to see. He was clearly able to identify that the many different judgements that he was putting on the work situation were spinning him around and around the washing machine of his thoughts. Once he was able to identify the fact that there hadn't been much time spent on his idea, this helped him to be more compassionate to himself and see that this was hurtful for him, without spinning further into his speculations about others' thoughts. Eric could also clearly see how important his work was to him and he decided to ask someone for feedback in terms of how he could improve his pitches.

Eric's 5-minute breakout

Eric's 5-minute breakout was two-fold. The first element involved him taking up to five minutes to recognise the judgements that he was placing on the situations that had occurred. The second element involved Eric taking five minutes daily when he had a big project to ask for feedback from trusted colleagues.

This small toward move generated very interesting and helpful feedback that was also hard for Eric to hear in the short term as it highlighted that he would benefit from doing more research and collaborating more with his peers. This was ultimately helpful for him and he is getting much more affirming responses, for the most part, at work since.

TODAY'S SMALL STEP

Choose one unblinkering strategy

Choose one of the strategies outlined in this chapter to practise unblinkering your perspective from the thoughts, judgements and stories your mind presents to you. Some strategies will work more effectively for you, depending on the challenges you're facing, so give both a go at some point and see how it works.

However, it is usually more helpful to commit to practising one strategy at a time. This way, it is easier to record in your small steps diary how useful your chosen strategy worked for you. Remember, the proof of the pudding is in whether you manage afterwards to engage in the small toward move that brings you one step closer to what is important to you.

23

More Ways to Unblinker the Monsters of Our Minds

Some of us think holding on makes us strong, but sometimes it is letting go. Hermann Hesse

In this chapter we provide some more unblinkering strategies that many of our clients and workshop attendees have found helpful. It's a good idea to read through this chapter in a few sittings, marking the strategies that resonate with you as you go along. The chapter is also a reference tool that can be returned to at any time.

1. Leaves on the stream

Imagine sitting on a riverbank and noticing that there's a tree beside you. Its leaves are falling from its branches, into the stream. Start to imagine that your thoughts are those leaves, floating down the stream. This isn't about trying to get rid of all the leaves or thoughts; it simply gives you a chance to notice your thoughts from an inner observer perspective. You need to be aware of your tendency to go up to the clouds, away from the exercise, or get right into the river among your thoughts. Bring yourself back to the observer perspective on the riverbank if and when you notice yourself in either of these two unhelpful modes. There is an MP3 of this exercise on our website.

Jimmy

Jimmy's mind always felt like it was racing. He was reluctant to try the leaves on the stream exercise at first because he was blinkered by the thought that he didn't have a good imagination. The first time he did the exercise, he was completely preoccupied with getting the exercise right, and as a result, became blinkered by the thought that 'this doesn't work for me'. When Jimmy realised that many people get blinkered by this thought, he was willing to give the exercise another go at home. On subsequent occasions, he put less pressure on himself to set the exercise up perfectly in his mind and allowed himself to notice his thoughts coming and going, neither running after his thoughts nor pushing them away.

After practising daily for a week, Jimmy was able to recognise his thoughts far more quickly and disentangle himself from unhelpful thinking patterns. He also discovered that he was able to fall asleep quicker at night as he was no longer caught up in the washing machine trap.

2. Change 'but' to 'and'

A good sign that we are blinkered is when we say things like, 'I'd love to do X, but I'm too anxious.' We encourage you to change this statement to: 'I'd love to do X, and I notice a lot of anxiety within me right now.' As best you can, notice where you use 'but' statements and change them to 'and' statements, focused on the present moment rather than sweeping generalisations.

Sophie

Sophie really wanted a promotion, yet being promoted would likely mean flying for work and public speaking – two things she was absolutely terrified of. Sophie would frequently say things like, 'I'm so bored of my job but I'm too anxious to fly so I'll have to stay where I am,' or 'I get really inspired when I watch TED talks but I know I could never do one because I'd go too red.' Sophie was encouraged to 'get off her buts', so whenever she noticed a 'but' she changed it to an 'and'. We are happy to report that she has got promoted. She was very anxious on her first few flights in particular and she did get red during one public speaking event; however, she is far happier on the whole in this job and thinks the small moments of anxiety are more than worth it.

3. Acknowledge the short-term gain

It's important to remember that every single thought we have and action we engage in makes sense. When a thought such as 'I'm overwhelmed' shows up, if you take it at face value, go along with this thought and let it dictate what you do and what you don't do, then what feelings, thoughts, or situations might this help you avoid or escape from in the short term?

If we are blinkered by the thought 'I'm overwhelmed', and let's say we're not happy with our job, we might not apply for a promotion or we might not apply for a new job. So in the short run going along with the thought helps us to avoid an interview. It helps us to avoid the potential rejection of not getting the job, yet in the long term it keeps us where we're not happy, and most likely even more overwhelmed.

Practice: Take a moment to settle in a chair, sitting in an alert position. As best you can, take five mindful breaths, with either your eyes closed or your gaze fixed, fully connecting to each inhalation and exhalation.

Give yourself a couple of minutes to reflect on what short-term gains you experience when you become blinkered by the unwanted thought, 'I'm overwhelmed'. What unwanted experiences and consequences can you avoid by letting this thought dictate your actions?

As best you can, bring compassion to your desire to avoid rejection, failure or any other unwanted experience. Finally, re-anchor in your values and actively choose a toward move that you will engage in when this unwanted thought arises.

Aleisha

Aleisha, like many of us, was plagued by the thought that she wasn't good enough. Initially she couldn't see any value or benefit in this thought, but when she explored it further, she realised that when she bought into the thought 'I'm not good enough', she avoided a lot of situations that had the possibility of failure or being rejected. Therefore, for her, the secondary gain of being blinkered by the thought, 'I'm not good enough', was a temporary postponing of the possibility of sadness or disappointment if failure or rejection occurred. Once she realised this, it was easier for her to have compassion and understanding for her thought, and she also discovered that the long term impact of being blinkered by this thought and letting it dictate her actions was a much smaller life than the one she wanted.

Since this realisation, Aleisha now notices her thought about not being good enough and sees that it's trying to help her by giving her some short-term gain, and she deliberately engages in toward moves such as joining a basketball team and attending a film club. Her thoughts of not being good enough still show up, but don't hold her back as much.

4. Tell yourself: 'I'm having the thought that. . . .'

Your mind tends to broadcast all the things it reckons you're not doing well. Dr Russ Harris termed this 'Radio Doom and Gloom'. It's a bit like an overprotective parent who's going a little too far. This process is called the negativity bias, whereby our mind disproportionately remembers things that it considers negative in a bid to keep us safe and protected, from an evolutionary perspective. Whereas in reality, this process often over activates our red alert threat system.

So, let's take, for example, the 'Radio Doom and Gloom' broadcast, 'I feel tired'. If you go along with that thought, buy into it and let it control you, where does that leave you? What do you get for buying into it? Often when we go along with that thought, we just start getting really tired. We say things like, 'I'll put it off; I'll do it another day instead.'

Remember, it's not about whether the thought is true or not true. We might actually *feel* tired. For example, you just completed a ten-and-a-half-hour flight, so your mind tells you that you're tired. But if you get really hooked on the thought, 'I'm tired', it will actually disconnect you from the people around you.

Many people struggle with thoughts like 'I'm useless' or 'I'm a failure'. When we succumb to the self-bullying thought that we're useless and/or a failure, we start backing away from things, making our lives smaller and smaller.

If you notice yourself getting caught up in a thought like 'I'm tired' or 'I'm useless' or 'I can't do that' or 'I'm a terrible partner or daughter or brother', you can just take a step back and say to yourself, 'I'm having the thought that I'm tired', or 'I'm having the thought that I can't do that', or 'I'm having the thought that I'm a terrible partner', or 'I'm having the thought that I'm getting this all wrong.'

This is not about trying to get rid of the thought or make it go away. It's simply about acknowledging it for what it is – a thought, nothing more and nothing less. This thought might be true and it might not be. We don't need to get overly caught up in debating its validity. We just want to acknowledge the thought, so that we're not blindly being pushed around by it.

The great thing about this unblinkering strategy is that it works really well with thoughts that are true as well as those that aren't, so in this way it's self-validation rather than self-bullying.

5. Repeat your thought very quickly

This unblinkering strategy involves repeating your thought quickly, over and over. So, for example, let's take the word 'failure', which most of us don't like to think about ourselves. When we hear the word failure, most of us have quite a strong, almost visceral, response. Many of us will feel tension or tightness in some part of our body.

Repeat the word really quickly, over and over again for 40 seconds, something like 'failure, failure …'. You will need to use a timer, as most of us think we've being doing this exercise for a minute when only ten seconds have passed.

You want to repeat it so quickly that you're not even able to hear the word anymore. You're just repeating it over and over again. Research has found that if you do this for 40 seconds or more, it generally reduces the impact of the word on you. What we're doing here is exposing ourselves to a word that we usually try and push away. When we actually say it over and over again very quickly, it loses a little bit of its power.

Michael

Michael had a massive fear of being perceived as a failure by himself and others. Whenever he heard the word, he would shudder and feel a tightness in his stomach. When this exercise was suggested to him, he became visibly uncomfortable and really didn't want to do it. However, he was able to identify that this aversion to the word failure was leading him to spread himself too thin and ultimately make mistakes, and sometimes even fail, in his desire to avoid failure. When he first said the word, he felt this throughout his entire body. He described it as his whole body being on red alert – tense and wound tight throughout, particularly around his head, neck and shoulders. When he repeated the word extremely quickly for 40 seconds, his body started to release some of its tension and he even cracked a smile half way into the exercise, something that he was definitely not expecting. Michael repeated this exercise twice a day for a week, and deliberately engaged in a toward move of slowing down and being more conscientious. He did less the following week, yet what he did do was of a much higher standard and he was more content with this.

6. Are you a passenger or the pilot?

Sometimes, it can feel like you are a passenger in your own life, at the beck and call of whatever thoughts are going through your mind. However, the only real power that your mind and thoughts have is in their power to intimidate you. A thought such as 'I'm overwhelmed' does not have the power to stop you doing whatever you're doing, even when it's valuable. In fact, many of us have had the thought about being overwhelmed and anxious before a job interview or an exam, and still gone ahead and done the interview or exam. At these times we felt like the pilot of our own lives.

Some of us, however, may have felt like a passenger in the past and given into such thoughts. This, too, is totally normal.

A small yet effective tool can be to ask yourself if you're being a passenger or a pilot in relation to your thoughts in any given moment. Your mind has the power to intimidate you into being a passenger, but the pilot's seat is always there for you.

Evelyn

Evelyn had a challenging childhood, to say the least. Her parents and other caregivers were not very responsive to her needs and they often told her that she was lazy or stupid. Perhaps unsurprisingly, Evelyn internalised these judgements and harsh narratives; so much so that often it felt like she was a passive passenger in her own life, where her comings and goings seemed to be dictated by the whimsical nature of her mind.

If she was feeling cheerful and optimistic about her life, she would engage in toward moves of connecting with others. If her mind was in a harsher mode, she would engage in away moves of avoiding other people and eating comfort food. Whether she was engaging in toward moves or away moves in the past, it always felt like her mind was in control. This changed, though, slowly but surely, when she started to actively question herself about whether she was the pilot or the passenger.

Evelyn pays attention to her thoughts, but for the most part they are passengers and she is the pilot. How this manifests practically is that she will sometimes go to an event for a shorter period of time when her passengers are acting up rather than avoiding the event altogether. She's often surprised that when she gets to an event, her passengers quieten down. However, this doesn't always happen and this isn't the point of the exercise. The point is that she is the pilot, and that gives her a lot more freedom and empowerment in her life.

7. Problem-solving

Let's say your mind is saying things like 'you're useless', 'you're a failure', 'you're angry, annoyed', 'you're tired'. This is your mind engaging in problem-solving. You're uncomfortable, so your mind tries to figure out a way to stop this discomfort. However, self-criticism is not a very effective solution.

So, if your mind tells you you're useless or a failure, it will also try to keep you from doing things that might result in you being called useless or that you might fail at. However, this will also keep you away from the engagements and activities that will actually break you out of thinking that you're useless or a failure.

A very effective practice involves simply acknowledging that your mind is trying to problem-solve. This can really help you understand that your mind is trying its best to protect you. It also gives you a chance to assess whether the solutions your mind is suggesting are in fact helpful or not.

If the solution your mind suggests is helpful, in that it brings us closer towards a rich and meaningful life, then you can engage in your toward move. However, since your mind often goes into self-protection mode, many of its attempts at solutions may involve an urge to engage in an away move. Recognising this, you can say to yourself, 'Here is my mind problem-solving. I acknowledge this, and would like to choose an action that is more in line with my values.'

This is far more effective than either blindly following your mind's suggestions or belittling your mind for the suggestions it has made. Your mind really was only trying to solve a problem.

8. Say your thought in a silly voice

We wouldn't advocate this small skill with all thoughts, such as traumatic thoughts or thoughts around your own or a loved one's illness. However, it can be very useful for some thoughts.

This skill works well with thoughts like 'things never work out for me' or 'it's always like this'. 'Always' and 'never' statements are rarely true, so it can be useful to imagine those in a silly voice. You can imagine your favourite cartoon character saying your thought in their usual voice with their usual mannerisms. If you have a smartphone, there's an app called Talking Tom, where you can say your thought and Talking Tom will repeat it back in a funny voice. The key here is that the cartoon is not trying to ridicule you or belittle your thought, it's about giving you a chance to see the thought from a different and lighter perspective.

Steven and Clodagh

Steven and Clodagh both attended a group around anxiety. They both decided to use the silly voice strategy when they were having unwanted thoughts such as 'you never have anything to say' and 'you always mess up'. They both care about relationships and connection. This is why much of their anxiety arises around social situations. They both said these thoughts into the Talking Tom app and heard them back in a silly voice.

After doing this, Steven started laughing. He finds it funny hearing Talking Tom say his thought back, and his anxiety is replaced by a feeling of happiness. He decides to stay at home and play computer games and feels relieved in the short term.

Clodagh, on the other hand, feels a spike in her anxiety after saying her thought into the Talking Tom app. She notices the thought, 'This is silly, I shouldn't be doing this exercise, there's something wrong with me.' Yet the process also gives her the chance to re-anchor in what's important to her — social connection and relationships — and she chooses to go out and meet her cousin even though she feels anxious in the short term. Clodagh ultimately feels better about her choices and herself in the long term.

Who do you think was truly unblinkered from the Power of Small perspective? Perhaps you guessed it. Clodagh. While it's totally natural for us to want to feel better and calm, the true gauge of our progress in this approach lies in our ability to reconnect to what is important and let this guide our actions, rather than our thoughts.

9. Name the story and access what matters to you

Often, we are not just blinkered by one thought. There can be a whole host of thoughts, frequently in the form of judgements, evaluations and comparisons, going on at any one time. It can be incredibly helpful to name this story, and to access what is meaningful to you amid this challenging situation.

In a challenging situation, by naming the story, you give yourself some space to connect with your inner values and intentions in relation to the situation. You can name your story and access what matters to you in five steps:

1. Write down all the unwanted judgements,

evaluations and comparisons you have about this challenging situation. Then fold this piece of paper.

2. On the front cover of your piece of paper, write, 'Here is the _____ story again!' to acknowledge the main theme for you. For example, fill in the blank space with 'not enough' or 'terrible family', or 'I'm overwhelmed'.

    (Note: It's important to encapsulate the name of the story in just two words. Sometimes clients will call their stories protracted things like 'people always let me down and I'm always left on my own in the end'. Now, that's a very long story title, and it will most likely make you more blinkered, rather than less. So, we could take that theme and reduce it to the 'let down' story or the 'distrustful me' story – something that summarises the main theme yet brings it down to two words.)

3. On the top part of the back cover, write down the three qualities you want to embody in this challenging situation, for example connection, compassion and courage. This is what truly matters to you.

4. On the bottom part of the back cover, write down three small actions you can take that would reflect these qualities. For example, taking three connected breaths, listening attentively, and responding

compassionately to a loved one. These are your small toward moves rooted in your values.

5. Carry this piece of paper around with you for the next week and notice when you are caught up in the content (A). Then bring yourself back to acknowledging the name of the story (B) and what's most important to you in relation to the story (C and D).

Lucy

Lucy was feeling extremely overwhelmed around the breakdown of her marriage. While she wouldn't judge others harshly around a marital relationship ending, she noticed that she was giving herself an incredibly hard time. Lucy seemed to flip between being caught in the pink elephant trap of trying not to think the thoughts, and the washing machine trap of being completely consumed by these thoughts. This was starting to have a massive impact on her closest relationships and her levels of attention in her job as a teacher.

Through coaching in this process, Lucy was able to identify the various different unwanted internal experiences that were arising within her, such as thoughts like 'I'm a failure because my marriage failed', emotions like shame and regret, and bodily sensations such as ongoing tension headaches and neck pain. When she looked at all the unwanted internal experiences together, she noticed an obvious theme, which was separation shame, so Lucy called this internal narrative the 'separation shame' story. This really helped her to unblinker from this internal narrative.

She further unblinkered herself by recognising her inner core values through asking herself what kind of person she wanted to be throughout the separation process. She identified 'connected to children', 'self-respecting' and 'open to friends' as core guiding principles for her. Once she'd acknowledged these, it was relatively straightforward to identify her toward moves, which involved taking at least ten to 15 minutes per day to deliberately make herself available, one to one, to each of her children; to give herself five to ten minutes per day to validate her unwanted emotions, which themselves were a natural and valid response to a marriage separation; and to text or call at least one friend per day, and meet at least one friend in person per week.

It is difficult to overstate how pivotal this process was for Lucy and her process of getting her life back on track after it had been derailed through an unexpected infidelity and separation. This took time, and Lucy looked at this story three times a day for 30 seconds to a minute at a time. At the start, it was a lot of effort, yet over time it became more habitual. Lucy's family and friends, and even her teenage sons, noticed that there was a renewed pep in her step.

10. Take your mind for a walk

It can be helpful to record yourself saying the various different thoughts your mind feeds you on an ongoing basis and then walking around for five minutes, listening to these thoughts on repeat. Once the five minutes are up, spend another five minutes walking around mindfully paying attention to your five senses. For many this is an unpleasant yet highly insightful experience, which really helps them to take their power back from their minds.

John Paul

John Paul, like many of us, was highly self-critical. He would go back over situations that had occurred in the recent past, and also years and decades before in a constant washing machine cycle. His mind was flooded with thoughts such as, 'why didn't I act differently in that relationship?' and 'I really messed up so bad at work' and 'I'm just such a loser'.

When the exercise of taking your mind for a walk was suggested, John Paul was not keen. He stated that he 'just wants to get away from' his mind. This was an indication that he was pendulum-swinging from the pink elephant trap to the washing machine trap. Once he understood that this exercise could help him gain a different perspective on his mind that might help him respond differently, he was willing to give it a go. He found the exercise challenging: he was saddened, like many others who do this exercise, to realise that he wouldn't talk to anyone else the way he speaks to himself. He was surprised to notice that when he listened to these thoughts out loud and repetitively, they started to sound a little silly or reduce in importance.

When he took time to connect to his five senses, he enjoyed seeing, hearing and feeling things that he often wouldn't fully see, hear and feel. Over the following weeks, John Paul was much better able to recognise when his mind was pendulum-swinging between the pink elephant and washing machine traps and to reconnect to his five senses. This helped him to be a lot more aware and attentive in his relationships. In fact, he started dating someone shortly after this exercise, and repeated the exercise when he noticed old fears re-emerging. He resisted his automatic tendency to press the eject button,and instead continued engaging in toward moves around compassion, care and attention to both himself and his boyfriend, which has been incredibly helpful for him.

11. Thank your mind

Let's say that your mind comes up with a thought like, 'If I don't do X then Y will happen'; for example, 'If I don't help this person out, then they'll never talk to me again.'

This unblinkering strategy involves genuinely thanking your mind for that thought. Say to yourself, 'Thank you, mind, I know you're trying to help me. You want me to have really solid relationships. You want to make sure I don't do something I'll regret. I really appreciate it; however, on this occasion I'm going to do something different.'

The idea is for you to recognise that your mind is trying to help you. Let's say your mind might be replaying a conversation that you had earlier. In this scenario, you could respond to your mind by saying, 'Thank you, mind, I know you're trying to help me right now. However, if I actually pay attention to you in this moment I won't be able to pay attention to what I'm doing. I hear what you're saying, yet I'm going to refocus my attention on the task at hand.'

12. Reality check

Ask yourself when you buy into a thought such as 'I'm overwhelmed', or give it all your attention, how do your actions change? What do you start or stop doing when this thought shows up? So, for example, with the thought 'I'm overwhelmed', when we give all our time and attention to the thought of being overwhelmed, often we'll revert to inaction, we'll start backing away from things so as not to exacerbate the sense of overwhelm further. So, we might start doing things like procrastinating and doing other tasks not related to our sense of overwhelm, and we might stop doing things like tackling the overwhelm head on, one small step at a time.

13. Physicalise your unwanted thought

A lot of people notice major resistance to this unblinkering skill when they hear of it first, yet they often get something from it. It can be helpful to either close your eyes or fix your gaze on the ground and reflect on what your unwanted thought would look like.

If you took the thought of 'I'm angry' or 'I'm annoyed', what would that thought look like? If it had a colour, what colour would it be? If it had a sound, what would it sound like? How big is it? Does it feel tiny or huge? Is the thought in your voice or someone else's?

Where does it feel like your thought is located in space? Is it in front of you, behind you, beside you or inside you? Is it moving or is it still? If it is moving, identify the direction and speed.

The aim of the exercise is not to derive any particular meaning, but to expose ourselves to the thought and see it from a different perspective so that it's less likely to blindside us. We're looking at it through a slightly different lens. We're usually so blinkered by our thoughts, or caught up in pushing them away, that we don't often get to look at them in new ways.

TODAY'S SMALL STEP

Practise one unblinkering strategy

Pick just one of our small skills for unblinkering from unwanted thoughts in this chapter, the one that appeals to you the most, and make an agreement with yourself to practise it when you are blinkered by unwanted thoughts over the coming week.

Remember, you can come back to this list time and time again to find new ways to respond to unwanted thoughts. Some strategies will be more helpful for certain challenging thoughts. There isn't one that works for everyone, yet everyone we've met so far can find at least one that works for them.

At a later date, it can be very helpful to experiment with some of the small strategies that are less appealing to you. We have found that people often get the most from those small strategies that they notice the most resistance to.

24
Emotional Traps

*Rather than letting our negativity get the better of us, we could
acknowledge that right now we feel like a piece of shit and not be
squeamish about taking a good look.* Pema Chödrön

Just as we can build up our psychological muscles by
responding to unwanted thoughts through the use of
unblinkering strategies, we can do the same in how we
respond to unwanted emotions.

How big, rich and meaningful your life will become
is directly related to the extent to which you are willing
and able to make room for unwanted emotions. If you're
unwilling to feel your feelings, it stands to reason that you
will always have to settle for a limited life, one that is smaller
than the one you dreamed of. So, the paradox is that it is
only through feeling your emotions that you can set yourself
free from being limited by them.

Before we detail some great small strategies for building a healthy relationship with unwanted emotions, let's explore the emotional traps we are all prone to falling into. There are some similarities with the thinking traps, and also some differences. And you'll discover that there are different small strategies for responding to unwanted feelings as opposed to thoughts.

The quicksand trap

If you fall into quicksand, how do you get out? The more you struggle against it, the further you'll get pulled into it, so is the answer to stop struggling? Not exactly.

If you stop struggling, you won't get pulled into the quicksand any further. However, you also won't get any further towards getting out. The only way to get out of quicksand is to lie back into it.

Imagine actually being swallowed alive by quicksand. Every bone in your body and every thought in your head would be telling you to try as hard as you could to get out of it, to fight for your life. But the only way out is totally counterintuitive, and it involves a lot of courage and trust.

This same process is relevant in terms of how we respond to unwanted emotions. The more we struggle with unwanted emotions, the further we get drawn into them. Sometimes, the only way through unwanted emotions and out the other side is to gather the trust and courage to make full contact with them.

The under the carpet trap

Another trap that many of us fall into is one that involves ignoring our emotions. We try to pretend that we are not having emotional reactions, or that aspects of our life, such as how others treat us, do not affect us. This is akin to seeing some dirt on our floor and just sweeping it under the carpet.

Obviously, it's not going to matter much if we shove the odd crumb under the carpet. However, the more stuff that we brush under there, the more overwhelming the hidden mess becomes. The mound of stuff we're trying to ignore can grow so high that we fall over the carpet and flat on our faces.

All of our emotional responses are important and valid. Ignoring or denying them has adverse consequences on a couple of fronts. First, we don't get a chance to acknowledge our emotional response and learn whatever it has to teach us. *All* emotions can teach us something, if we just pause to listen. Secondly, by ignoring or denying our emotions we invalidate them, which often leads to them intensifying over time. Our unwanted emotions grow in size and impact upon us more and more. In the next chapter, we'll revisit David, who you met earlier in the book, and see just how big and overwhelming our emotions can get when we continuously try to sweep them under the carpet.

The over-identification trap

On the flipside of ignoring or denying our emotions and

pushing them under the carpet, sometimes we may fall into the trap of over-identifying with them. We may notice ourselves describing or labelling ourselves as depressed, anxious, overwhelmed, or a worrier. In a hospital, a patient doesn't describe himself to a doctor as a cracked rib, or a broken arm, or cancer. Yet how often do we describe ourselves by how we are feeling inside?

When we get caught in this trap, we start to justify our actions and inactions with our emotions. We may notice ourselves saying things like, 'Well, I'd love to go on that weekend away but I'm just too anxious, so I wouldn't enjoy it anyway,' or, 'I couldn't possibly go to that party. I'm way too depressed to be socialising.'

We are not for a moment saying that anxiety and depression don't exist or that they don't adversely affect people. Indeed, they are conditions that we have both experienced personally, and so we speak from both personal and professional experience in saying that we will run into major problems when we consistently over-identify with our emotional state, allowing it to dictate what we do and do not do. The ultimate aim is to continually take small steps towards your values and engage in meaningful actions, which are independent of the mood you are in.

The deep-end trap recap

Similar to when you are working with unwanted thoughts through unblinkering, if you jump right into the deep end using these strategies, you have less chance of them helping you to swim. In fact, you increase your chances of drowning in your emotions.

So, it's best to start off small. The rule of thumb, as always, is to break out of your comfort zone little by little, while staying within your self-care zone.

Breaking out of emotional traps

As with the small skills we taught you for unblinkering from thoughts, there isn't one small skill that helps everyone to break out of their emotional traps. It can be a case of trial and error at the start.

It is important to note that using some of these skills may make you feel worse before you feel better. In fact, the aim here isn't about making you feel better, as in making you feel happier or calmer. It is to help you *feel more fully* what is going on in the moment. In this way, you can allow emotions to be your teachers for a better life.

The harsh reality is that if these strategies felt good, there would be no need for psychologists, coaches or self-help books. However, because they can be challenging to practise, while at the same time there is a whole host of small away moves that feel seductively good in the short term, many of us choose the pleasure and reassurance of short-term gain at the cost of long- term pain.

We are firm believers in Maya Angelou's words, 'We all do the best we can until we know better. Once we know better, then we can do better.' We find that it's best to treat these small strategies like an experiment, where you simply give them a go and notice what your experience is. If you go into them expecting yourself to feel better, or at least less bad, you will most likely get caught up in the quicksand trap. There are MP3s of these exercises on our website if you would prefer to be guided through them as an audio exercise.

Before you start engaging in these strategies, take the time to . . .

1. Acknowledge that your emotions contain important information.

2. Rather than demonising your unwanted emotions, recognise that they indicate a reality gap – a distinction between what your life is and what you would like your life to be. This indicates that change would in fact be helpful.

3. Acknowledge what happens when you move away from unwanted emotions.

4. While most of our default strategies are to say no to unwanted emotions, such as sadness, anxiety and resentment, there are often hidden costs to this. Check in with yourself and try, as best you can, to recognise what your default away moves are. How do you distract, opt out or use some form of self-defeating actions to avoid certain feelings? What are the short- and long term effects of these away moves?

5. Acknowledge what happens when you move towards your unwanted emotions.

6. It seems counterintuitive, yet it is often most helpful when we say yes to our unwanted emotions, mindfully moving towards them. Recognise what happens when you actively approach an unwanted emotion. What do you think are the short- and long term effects of these toward moves?

TODAY'S SMALL STEP

Motivation to spring emotional traps

In the next chapter, we will outline a number of small skills for springing emotional traps. To maximise your motivation to engage in this process fully, go through the six-step process outlined above.

You can do this either through some quiet reflection away from your usual distractions or through writing in your small steps diary.

25

Small Skills for Springing Emotional Traps

The boundary to what we can accept is the boundary to our freedom. Tara Brach

In this chapter, we will revisit David, who earlier in the book was working through his social anxiety around dating. When you last met David he was gradually moving out of his back away, not today mode of avoiding dating apps and opportunities to meet a potential partner when he believed he'd messed up. However, like many of us, David needed to spring many emotional traps in his quest to find a partner that felt like a good fit for him.

To help you to understand how you might be able to use these skills in your life, we will look at them through David and his struggles with emotions in the context of relationships.

Emotional avoidance

We all experience an unwillingness to feel certain emotions. Some will avoid conflict so as not to be around anger. Others may keep busy if they fear that when they stop, the sadness of a recent upset or loss will overcome them. And being the social creatures that we are, a particularly uncomfortable emotion for most of us to feel is shame.

David was expanding his comfort zone on dates by choosing to take more steps towards connecting and initiating meaningful conversation. He began to make real progress and started to build a deeper connection with Clare, who he'd had a few dates with. David was really pleased, very fond of Clare and excited to see where the relationship could go, but he was also feeling more and more anxiety each time they met.

When David investigated his anxiety around dating in session, it emerged that it revolved around a need to control situations so as to avoid feeling shame. As David put himself out there, and took more steps towards his values, he was becoming overwhelmed by the impossibility of avoiding shame. By taking more steps outside his comfort zone, putting himself into more social interactions and meeting more people, he also immediately increased his chances of messing up, saying the wrong thing and feeling uncomfortable emotions as a result. No matter how consciously he used the skills he had learned and put them into practice as best he could, he still got things wrong and messed up with his date.

If David said something awkward, made a clumsy joke, or forgot something important from a previous date, he felt a huge surge of embarrassment. Instantly, he felt his face redden and his body perspiring. Worried that he would have a panic attack, on one date he got up and left the table in the middle of a conversation over dinner. Other times, when his fear of shame became unbearable, he'd make his excuses and end a date abruptly. He didn't stick around to find out how the date would have gone, and he never brought these events up with Clare to gain her perspective. David was convinced he was failing and that Clare would dump him any day.

Pivoting an action from one designed to avoid what we fear towards one intended to bring us closer to our values can be a real challenge, when this very action could also bring us face to face with what we fear the most. Faced with this prospect, many of us will settle for unhelpful and self-defeating actions aimed at minimising our emotional suffering. Over time, relying on these control and avoidance strategies is exhausting and, in many cases, damaging.

Emotional flexibility

The true freedom to choose how to respond in the face of challenges lies in cultivating emotional flexibility, so that you can respond regardless of the direction in which your emotional avoidance strategies are pushing you. The power to act independently of emotional urges, frees you up to respond directly and helpfully to the need the feeling is alerting you to, rather than reacting to the urges to make the feeling go away. Reacting in this way may make the feeling temporarily subside, but if you never get to look at the underlying needs and problems, the emotion will continue to alert you again and again, because that's its job.

At one point, David was about to quit dating and close himself off again. At the last minute he'd cancelled a date he'd arranged with Clare, and had been ignoring her calls and texts since then, due to his embarrassment. David really liked Clare and knew he was probably blowing his chances, but he also experienced a strong urge to avoid feeling shame at all costs. He faced up to the dilemma of whether to run for the hills, away from anxiety and shame, or to reach out to Clare and accept the full range of emotions this would bring.

David needed to work on building his emotional flexibility so that his actions in response to challenging situations were in line with his values, and not dictated by an urge to push away his unwanted emotions. David worked through each of the three key ingredients of psychological flexibility, as described in Small Basics, applying them to his emotions.

1. Awareness of the present moment

When David's anxiety kicked in, his mind jumped to all the worst-case scenarios of how things would work out with Clare. Feeling defeated and hopeless, he would then shut down and withdraw emotionally and physically. By using skills aimed at bringing him more into contact with his emotions, thoughts and actions in the present moment, David was eventually able to stand back and see things more clearly.

Gaining this sense of perspective, David identified that while his mind was generating endless thoughts and images of an imagined future, in reality he could never truly know for sure how things would go. Being able to non-judgementally look at the thoughts, feelings and urges as they arose in the moment, David could distinguish more readily his fear-based version of future events from what he truly wanted. Despite the fear that he would make a fool of himself and potentially be rejected, he knew deep down that he would regret not doing everything he could to make it work with Clare. Once he identified clearly how his avoidant actions were impacting his life, he was equally determined not to close himself off again, as he pictured how small and empty his life looked.

In this chapter we will be looking at a variety of ways to help you connect more to your emotions, if you would like to practise these skills yourself. You can review the chapters on unblinkering to help you acknowledge and unblinker from unwanted thoughts, and review your toward and away moves to connect with your actions, at any time. The skills covered in Chapter Twenty-One, 'Tuning in to Your Five Senses', will give you a host of other ways to increase your awareness of the present moment.

Here are some of the specific skills David used to spring his emotional traps which you can try for yourself.

Objectify your emotion

Imagine the challenging emotion you are feeling is an object. Is it liquid, solid or gaseous? How big is it? Is it light or heavy? What temperature is it? What shape does it have? What colour? Is it transparent or opaque? What does its surface feel like? Hot or cold? Rough or smooth? Wet or dry?

The answers here aren't that important. It's more that this exercise can help you increase your ability to be able to stay with the feeling rather than get caught up in it.

When David objectified his emotions, be broke out of the under the carpet and quicksand traps. Up until then, he'd been pushing his emotions under the carpet, but the constant struggle of this led to him being swallowed up in them as a result. Through doing this exercise, he learned that he could acknowledge and stay with his emotions, even if that was uncomfortable.

Find daily emotional space

Would you be willing to stop for five minutes each day for a week to create some space to acknowledge your emotions exactly as they are? This practice allows you to look under the carpet and acknowledge your emotions rather than letting them build up into something overwhelming, which can seem completely unbearable and unmanageable.

It's important to acknowledge that the time required each day is going to be different at different points of our lives. If somebody is in the early stages of grief or bereavement, more time may be needed to allow space for the attendant emotions. However, small check-ins with your emotions are vital. Allowing that small emotional space every day is a helpful way to keep in touch with your emotions in a real way.

This daily practice helped ensure that David didn't go back into shoving his feelings under the carpet where they could build up, and that he maintained the benefits he'd experienced after objectifying his feelings.

2. Openness to experience challenging emotions

If you have a tendency to close down or withdraw when you encounter challenging emotions, the invitation for you is to open up and make room in your life for whatever you happen to be experiencing, as you're experiencing it. This is essentially what acceptance is all about – to make room for whatever we experience and let it be, without trying to change, control or get rid of it. For David, this involved him building up his capacity to experience shame without it getting in the way of him being open and honest about his challenges, rather than letting shame press the eject button on his interactions.

When David started rebuilding his relationship with Clare, each step brought up uncomfortable and unwanted emotions. Before he called her, he was nauseous and shaky. Previously, this would have rung alarm bells for him to run away, but instead he phoned her.

When David was getting ready to meet Clare face to face, his head fed him images of it all going horribly wrong. At one point on his journey to meet her, the anxiety felt so unbearable, he pulled the car over, but he didn't follow the strong urge to turn back home. And when it came time to explain his recent actions to Clare, he sat through the fear and shame and opened up to her finally.

David was able to face unwanted experiences he had never faced before and work through the emotions he had avoided at all costs to make meaningful change to his actions. Here are some skills you can use to help build your flexibility to stay with difficult emotions, while moving towards something that matters to you.

Breathe in to your body

When you're feeling strong unwanted emotions, it can be incredibly grounding to place one hand at the level of your heart and one hand at the level of your stomach. Often, when we are overwhelmed and stressed up to our eyeballs, we start to breathe quite shallowly. So, it's best to aim to move your chest and stomach so that you can feel your hands rising and falling with your breath. These deeper breaths will activate your safety system.

It can also be helpful to imagine that you are breathing into a balloon in your stomach to help your breath deepen when strong emotions are present.

David would engage in this exercise before he called or met Clare. He found it helpful to call her from his mobile phone headset so that he could keep his hands on his chest and stomach as a compassionate support to himself throughout the call. When out at restaurants, he would sometimes consciously connect to his breath when he noticed his old urges to run emerge.

Drop the struggle

Imagine you are holding a rope and that both hands are trying to pull the rope in different directions. What do you think is going to happen to your time, energy and resources if you continue to engage in this tug-of-war with yourself?

Often when we have an unwanted emotion, we engage in a similar tug-of-war. However, it's helpful to remember that whenever you are struggling against an unwanted emotion, you are really struggling against yourself.

As best you can, experiment with dropping this struggle and noticing how this affects your time, energy and resources.

David physically used a scarf and spent one minute pulling the scarf in different directions. This helped him to fully realise just how futile his attempts were, and the exhausting impact they were having on his time and energy. David then listened to a short recording on a daily basis, where he would reconnect to the struggle he had experienced when fighting with himself, and the relief he experienced when he let go of this struggle. This allowed him to reconnect with his inner core values. You can find this recording, and recordings for many other exercises, on our website.

The 'drop the struggle' metaphor was incredibly helpful

for David. He started to say to himself, 'Oh there I go again struggling; just drop the struggle.' He was surprised by how effective this was for him. Through this action, he broke out of the quicksand trap instantly. In those moments, he would come back to connecting with Clare.

Engage in active acceptance

David often did the following exercise (which we outlined in Chapter 20, 'Let Things Get a Little Messy') before meeting Clare, or after a date if he was giving himself a hard time. Again and again, it would help him to move out of the trap of being overidentified with his thoughts and emotions, towards acknowledging them as only one part of his experience. In order to avoid the deep-end trap, David used fairly mundane scenarios at first when practising this skill, and slowly built up to the situations where he felt the most shame and embarrassment.

3. Engagement in what really matters rather than escaping

David's core value centred around leaning in towards what was important, and doing everything within his power to repair his relationship – even if this meant experiencing the challenging emotions he had been working so hard to avoid.

Make a deliberate different action

Most of us have our go-to actions when we feel an unwanted emotion. Some of us are going to be more prone to opting out, engaging in away moves like procrastination, cancelling plans, and going to bed. Some of us will be more prone to distraction, engaging in away moves like eating chocolate, binge-watching Netflix or overscheduling our time. And many of us will use a combination of these actions in different pivotal valued areas in our lives.

We invite you to engage in deliberate different action. For somebody who generally distracts and keeps themselves busy, deliberate different action might involve slowing down – taking a moment to pause rather than reaching for the distraction. If you are someone who usually goes underneath the duvet and gets completely overwhelmed by the emotion, deliberate different action might involve spending five minutes really actively connecting to the unwanted emotion.

Through engaging in deliberate different action, we will get closer to the middle path.

Through continued deliberate different action and the other skills outlined here, David repaired his relationship with Clare, and they continued to date for a few months until she moved to London for work. At first, this came as a big knock to David. The relationship had been going really well. David felt more comfortable in his own skin with another person than he ever had before. They chatted about a long-distance relationship, and David was tempted. However, by continuing to work actively on his emotional flexibility, he realised ultimately that this would be an away move to stop the pain of breaking up and the fear of being on his own again. When he connected with what he truly wanted, the toward move was for him to move on and try to find someone who lived closer and wanted to settle in his hometown.

David is continuing to utilise the emotional flexibility skills he learned when facing his fears with Clare, and committing to dating according to his values. He continues to practise the skills in this chapter to spring emotional traps. He is navigating the world of dating a lot more consciously, and in a way that is increasingly filled with toward moves.

TODAY'S SMALL STEP

Springing emotional traps

Most of us need a combination of skills in order to spring out of our under the carpet, quicksand and over-identification traps. We encourage you to pick one small skill first and practise this at least three times before moving on to another. Track your progress in your small steps diary.

26

Attend, Investigate and Release Feelings in the Body

Freedom is not given to us by anyone; we have to cultivate it ourselves. It is a daily practice . . . No one can prevent you from being aware of each step you take or each breath in and breath out. Thich Nhat Hanh

In the last chapter, we looked at various ways to spring emotional traps. Here, we will address how to work with particularly intense unwanted emotions in more detail. Emotions are essentially events in the body, and while you may not be able to control them directly, whenever and wherever you want, you can help to regulate them.

Emotions, no matter how excruciating or long-lasting they feel, all rise and then fall again. If we allow them to run their course through our bodies, while turning our attention to what we can learn from them before they pass, we can respond with meaningful and authentic toward moves.

Emotion and bodily wisdom

When you're overwhelmed by intense emotions that feel like they're flooding your body, it can be really tempting to jump to the short-term fix by reacting from one of your D.O.T.S. pain-avoiding strategies (distraction, opting out, thinking traps and self-defeating actions). However, what you're experiencing internally is showing up for a reason. If you can practise mindfully connecting with these vital sources of information in your body, you can harness the knowledge and understanding required to take effective action in order to resolve; not the emotion itself, but the underlying issue the emotion is trying to alert you to.

The trouble sometimes is that our minds get in the way of this natural process; our thoughts and judgements about the emotion keep re-firing it, like striking a drum, again and again. Focusing directly on your bodily sensations helps you sidestep your reasoning mind.

It will be useful later to analyse and problem-solve around what prompted the emotion, but when responding to intense emotions, it's best to leave the head out of it until the body has a chance to recalibrate. The last thing your emotions need is explaining or rationalising. At this point, the most helpful action you can take is to accept your emotions and validate them as best you can.

When emotions feel particularly intense, or when there are too many emotions to handle at one time, it can be difficult to focus on anything else. We teach our clients to use what we call the 'AIR system' to connect with their bodies when they feel like their emotions have them in a headlock.

A – Attend

I – Investigate

R – Release

A – Attend

1. Pause and connect with the challenging emotion or sensation showing up for you in the moment.

2. Observe any labels or judgements from your mind about the emotion, for example 'this is too much', 'I need to get rid of this', 'this is bad'.

3. Notice also any urges you experience to push away or get rid of the emotion with an away move, for example reaching for the biscuits, sending a strongly worded email, or opening a bottle of wine.

I – Investigate

1. Describe the emotion as best you can, in particular how it manifests in your body, for example heaviness in your chest, tightness in your shoulders, a queasy sensation in your tummy, etc.

2. Lean in a little closer to what the emotion or sensation is trying to communicate to you. What is it trying to tell you about what is important to you in this moment?

3. How can you use this information to engage in an action that will bring you closer to what is important?

R – Release

1. Once you can acknowledge your emotions and sensations, and listen to what they are signalling, thank them for alerting you to your needs and guiding you to what you needed to do.

2. Now see if you can expand inside to make as much room as possible for this emotion. Focus your breathing to breathe in and around the part of your body where you feel these sensations most intensely – your chest, maybe, or your stomach – and see if you can release the area a little more with each breath.

3. Open your mind, soften your heart, and set your intention to release the emotion or sensation from your body.

Acceptance isn't something that we can just turn on in the moment. It is something we need to continually practise over time, just as a healthy diet and exercise plan needs to be consistent in order to maintain your fitness and shape. The more you practise leaning in to your emotions, over time they will lose their power to overwhelm you or dictate your actions. Emotions can become something you have, that come and go, rather than something you are.

TODAY'S SMALL STEP

Practise AIR

Practise the steps of AIR and track your experience in your small steps diary, describing as best you can what you observed and experienced. Note any differences from how you usually respond to this emotion.

27

From Wilfulness to Willingness

If someone comes along and shoots an arrow into your heart, it's fruitless to stand there and yell at the person. It would be much better to turn your attention to the fact that there's an arrow in your heart . . . . Pema Chödrön

One of the most subtle away moves that many of us get caught up in is operating from old, internalised scripts. Rather than choosing to respond in challenging situations from a toward perspective, we get caught up in what we think is right, just or fair.

Often what we consider to be right, just and fair is a product of our learning and life histories so far, in which all of our previous experiences have become jumbled up to form our opinions, perspectives and views about the world. A small, yet ever so important, shift that we can make is one from wilfulness to willingness, gradually expanding our limiting and rigid perspectives to more expansive and life-enhancing ones.

Wilfulness

Most of us find it easier to spot wilfulness in others than in ourselves. When we are wilful, we are generally hell-bent on being right and saving face. Wilfulness arises in relationships when we refuse to take any responsibility for our part in an argument or misunderstanding. Or it comes in the form of hanging on to a grievance long after the person has apologised because of 'the principle'. If the other person involved is also wilful, arguments can go on for days, weeks, months, years or sometimes even decades.

Wilfulness raises its head in the workplace when we refuse to ask for help because we don't want to appear incompetent. As a result, we may make a number of mistakes, which actually lead to the outcome we were afraid of – we appear incompetent.

Wilfulness shows up in the area of health and wellbeing when we refuse to engage in actions that we know, or have been told, will be helpful for our health and wellbeing. It might be continuing to live a sedentary lifestyle and eat high levels of sugary, stodgy foods, even though we have a heart problem. Or it could involve continuing to isolate ourselves and not do mindfulness or other psychological exercises that we have been recommended for our psychological wellbeing, even though we know we really need them.

Willingness

Willingness is at the opposite end of the spectrum to wilfulness, but it is a difficult pill for many of us to swallow because it usually asks that we also accept our own vulnerability.

Vulnerability is something that we're generally far more accepting of in others than in ourselves. In fact, many of us will guard our own vulnerability with our lives, and engage in numerous away moves aimed at hiding it, even from ourselves. Willingness starts with being open to sitting with, and fully experiencing, even the most painful of emotions, thoughts and sensations.

Willingness in relationships looks like making the first attempt to make amends, if you know that you had your fair part to play in an argument. Or if you're the kind who generally apologises, even for things that are not your fault, it could mean standing up for yourself in a compassionate, yet assertive, manner.

Willingness in work involves admitting when you're wrong, or when you've made mistakes, or being willing to ask for help, even when your inner critic says you shouldn't, in case people think you're incompetent.

Willingness in health and wellbeing involves being open to doing what is best for you, even though it may be uncomfortable. This involves taking an honest look at your habits, and taking responsibility for changing the habits that are making or keeping you unwell, either physically or psychologically. It takes tremendous courage and willingness to change what may seem like the habits of a lifetime.

Small moves towards willingness

Through continued shifts from wilfulness to willingness, your life expands, one toward move at a time. Wilfulness is seductive. It can feel good to give in to stubborn urges in the short term, yet ultimately this is unhelpful in terms of our long term dreams and aspirations. Willingness, on the other hand, involves playing the long game and focusing on what is needed in a situation at that moment, and deciding which battles to keep for another day.

So, rather than getting right into it with a loved one in the heat of an argument, wait and practise willingness to come back to the argument at a later point, when the other person is more likely to actually hear what you have to say, and when you have calmed down sufficiently to say it in a less incendiary way.

Willingness involves doing what is helpful and workable, rather than what your mind tells you is right, fair or just. It is about being open to feeling unwanted emotions, working with challenging thoughts, and sitting with uncomfortable bodily sensations.

With willingness practice, we can develop an openness to allowing life experiences to be our teacher. Our experiences, rather than our minds, dictate what we do and do not do in a variety of small ways which, taken together, have a massive impact on our lives. We become willing to adapt our perspective to fit the situation life presents us with, and to change or persist in our small actions in order to engage in the most meaningful action.

Shifting perspectives

An extremely useful small skill to help you develop willingness is to start to look at challenges in your life from different perspectives. Often when there is an unwanted or challenging situation arising in the moment, our defence system is activated. As a result, we often rely on very primitive ways of problem-solving internally, which are all about damage limitation and saving face.

Many of these primitive solutions will help us feel better in the short term, but will most likely make us feel a whole lot worse in the long run. Shifting perspectives is an amazing way of helping us make the best decision for ourselves, and thus gradually grow our willingness muscle. Any of the skills below can be used when you are experiencing a challenging situation, or finding it difficult to approach a situation with full willingness. There are expanded audio versions of these exercises on our website.

Five small exercises to shift perspective

1. Imagine that your best friend is in the exact same situation as you. What guidance would you give to your friend from a place of awareness, courage and love? Would you be willing to follow this guidance yourself?

2. Choose someone you know whose guidance you trust as being solid, fair and wise. Now, imagine that they can see the situation you're in and that they give you guidance from their solid, fair and wise perspective. Follow through on their guidance.

3. Connect to an older, wiser you, ten years from now. This you has been through all that you've been through and more, and they've come out the other side. Write a short letter of guidance from this older, wiser you to the you that is right here and now, struggling with this situation. Follow through on this guidance.

4. Imagine that the situation you were struggling with (as far as it is applicable) was happening to a child under ten that you know. What guidance would you give to this child? Would you be willing to follow this guidance yourself?

5. Take a moment to visualise how this situation is likely to move you towards or away from what really matters to you in the short, medium and long term, if you respond in a) a willing way or b) a wilful way. Make your decision about what to do next in line with what is likely to bring you the best long term outcome.

TODAY'S SMALL STEP

Practise small shifts in your perspective

Choose one of the shifting perspectives exercises above to develop your willingness muscle. Some exercises will be more suitable to particular challenges. The key here is to identify and engage in one small willingness action after you do the perspective shift.

28

From Shame to Compassion

Shame corrodes the very part of us that believes we are capable of change. Brené Brown

You're not always going to get it right, and life will most definitely not go to plan. Even when you're making a toward move, there are no guarantees it will be easy. The more you take the opportunities life invites you to say yes to, it statistically follows that you also open yourself up to getting some things wrong and messing up. Although your internal overprotective parent might scream at the mere notion of this, these experiences could be valuable for shifting the direction of your life. If you review these difficult experiences, and work with the discomfort brought up in you, you can use what you learn in your next toward move.

The shame cycle

Often, self-criticism and shame block us from ever really looking honestly and openly at ourselves. We cringe and struggle against our mistakes, and as if this wasn't painful enough, we then beat ourselves up repeatedly, often years after the event. Over time, we get caught in shame cycles, repeating the same unhelpful patterns without learning any other way of responding to our mistakes.

We evolved to self-criticise so that we could learn from our mistakes and adjust what we were doing, to give us the best chances of survival. The research is clear that self-reflection and self-acceptance are incredibly powerful, in terms of helping us to grow and develop in small yet meaningful ways. Self-criticism and shame have the opposite effect. The more we beat ourselves up for not living up to impossibly high standards, the more we go into extreme ways of responding.

The two opposite extremes of this spectrum are either completely overextending ourselves to the point of burnout (do-do, go-go), or backing away altogether from life and the challenges and opportunities it brings (back away, not today). By defining ourselves through our perceived mistakes and inadequacies, we inadvertently lock ourselves into a shame cycle of repeating the same pattern of away moves again and again. Our lives can begin to feel like a broken record.

Some examples of self-criticism and shame in action:

* Ari is preoccupied with appearing competent in his role as trainee accountant. He doesn't want to ask

questions because he's afraid it will make him look like he doesn't know what he's doing. When he does make mistakes he starts to criticise himself: 'I bet no other trainees makes these kinds of mistakes. Maybe I'm not meant to be an accountant. I'm just a fraud. People will get sick of me and I'll lose this job.' The more Ari criticises himself, the further he falls into the shame cycle. As a result, he is even less likely to ask for help the next time he needs it, making it more, rather than less, likely that he'll fall into the same trap again.

* Louise has struggled with her size for years. She desperately wants to get down to a healthy weight. Whenever she has a rough day, or even a lesser disappointment that brings up discomfort in her, she reaches for a big tub of Nutella and whatever sources of sugar are in the house.

   As she starts to eat, the self-criticism grows: 'Look at you, you fat slob. You'll never get slim as long as you do this, you lazy thing. You've got no self-control. How could anyone love you when you clearly can't take care of yourself?'

   The more Louise chastises herself, the worse she feels. In shame mode, she defines herself by her away moves. This becomes a vicious circle in which she feels worse and worse about herself. She continues to reach for her sugar crutch, which keeps the shame cycle alive.

✱ Liliana joined a drama class to meet new people and overcome her fear of public speaking. However, when she is required to do a scene, her mind frequently goes blank. Or if she does remember her lines, she later berates herself because her inner critic tells her that she did a terrible job: 'You're a terrible actress. You fluffed that line and it ruined the whole scene. If you can't do this, how the hell do you think you'll be able to deliver a presentation at work? You're even worse at this than you imagined.'

When Liliana gets caught in this spin cycle of shame, she disengages from her class. She becomes completely self-absorbed in her thoughts, and as a result doesn't take in what she is being taught. She starts to skip classes and tries to find ways out of public speaking in her work.

Compassion: the antidote to shame

Research has found that compassion is helpful in reducing shame, stress, anxiety and depression. This involves recognising our own suffering and being willing to alleviate it.

Through practising compassion-focused techniques and exercises, you can learn to develop your own internal caregiving system, which can help bolster you through difficulties and challenges. This practice is particularly helpful for those really squirmy things that tend to trigger a lot of shame or knock you into being very self-critical.

The three types of compassion

There are three main areas of compassion: self-to-self compassion, self-to-other compassion, and other-to-self compassion. Ideally, our lives will feature each of these three. Let's look at them in a little more detail.

1. Self-to-self compassion

Like it or not, like yourself or not, you are always going to be the protagonist in your own life. Your relationship with yourself inevitably affects your health and wellbeing, your relationships with others, your sense of contribution and purpose, and whether you allow yourself the chance to have fun or appreciate some downtime. Most of us were raised in settings where we were not taught how to develop healthy, loving and nurturing self-to-self relationships. Many of us witnessed our parents and others sacrificing their own needs for the sake of meeting another's.

Most of us can recall people at opposite ends of the spectrum – people who almost always put others' needs before their own, and those who almost always put their own needs first, with little or no regard for those around them. Neither end of this spectrum is particularly healthy or conducive to solid and meaningful long term relationships, either with ourselves or others.

When we frequently put others' needs before our own in a variety of small yet consistent ways, we give ourselves the message loud and clear that other people are more important than us, and that our needs don't matter. Through consistently brushing our own needs under the carpet, our unmet needs can build up and be expressed through passive-aggressive acts, or we can end up burned out, with little more left to give.

On the other end of the equation, if we are always meeting our own needs and neglecting the needs of others, we will often get the message, both externally from others and internally from ourselves, that we are selfish and that we can't cope with much in life besides taking care of ourselves.

A compassionate self-to-self relationship involves self-awareness, self-reflection and self-acceptance. We need to be aware of our own strengths and challenges. We need to recognise those times when lightening up on ourselves and taking some downtime is required, and also those times when we are coasting and could really do with expanding our comfort zones. We need to reflect daily on our small toward and away moves as each of these actions and inactions build up the tapestry that is our lives. We need to develop an acceptance of what is outside of our control and a willingness to take every small action that we can to make our life tomorrow better than our life today.

Self-to-self compassion for Ari would involve becoming aware that his need to appear always competent makes sense given his unique life history. Ari's parents were into keeping up appearances. There were times when they struggled financially, but they would never make this obvious to others. Ari and his siblings were taught to be self-sufficient and never show weakness. When his mother struggled with depression, this was always kept under wraps. When Ari and his siblings struggled with their feelings, their father was quick to point out that 'they didn't get that from his side of the family'.

Ari internalised all these rules for living from the various small things that his parents did and did not do, say and didn't say, ask and didn't ask. He learned to notice his tendency to hold back from appearing vulnerable, and the strong feeling of threat that was activated within him whenever he went to ask a question about something he didn't know or understand. He learned to self-soothe in a way that he had not been taught growing up, and then to engage in the tougher action – asking the question – rather than staying locked in his shame cycle.

2. Self-to-other compassion

Self-to-other compassion involves us recognising suffering in others and alleviating this suffering to the best of our abilities. Obviously, others' reactions are to a certain extent outside of our control; however, we do have a choice in terms of how we respond to others in the first place.

Nowadays, we are becoming increasingly self-focused. Granted this self-focus is generally not self-compassionate, but sometimes we can become numb or blind to the humanity of others. Just take a look at the scathing comments on social media and news sites to see what we mean.

We are becoming increasingly quick to judge, criticise and condemn others. In doing so, we deny a part of our – and their – common humanity. We start to divide the world into us versus them and in so doing, we lose contact with compassion for these other people and indeed for ourselves.

If we work on increasing compassion for others, we start to see fellow human beings in a broader, kinder and more understanding manner. Rather than seeing people as simply objects on which we can discharge whatever harsh judgements we like, we start to see one another as fellow travellers. This small, yet rather profound, shift helps us to build better relationships not only with others, but with ourselves. We begin to see others' perspectives and understand where they are coming from, thereby endorsing our own humanity.

In our practice we have facilitated groups and workshops where people come together because they share psychological struggles, be this with depression, anxiety, OCD, bipolar, addictions, or an increasing burden of overwhelm that doesn't fit neatly into a diagnostic category.

The vast majority of people who come to see us have high levels of shame. They find it hard to identify what is loveable and worthy about themselves. They have also learned to become quite critical and judgemental of the world due to one too many small, yet pervasive, reactions from others that led to them feeling inferior in some way.

As the group workshops progress, the attendees begin to

share more and more with one another. As they share in this safe and compassionate environment, they naturally develop a stronger muscle in terms of their self-to-other compassion. And as they extend compassion to others who are going through similar struggles to themselves, they slowly but surely, little by little, start to develop more self-to-self compassion also.

Louise really benefited from self-to-other compassion. She noticed that she was not only judgemental of her own weight and attitude towards food, she was also constantly monitoring other people's weight and what they were and weren't eating. She told her friends that they looked well when they'd lost a few pounds and wouldn't make any comment if they'd gained a few pounds.

Louise would frequently look through glossy magazines and form favourable opinions of those she deemed to be slim, and less favourable ones for those she considered to be overweight. As Louise learned to ease up on her judgements and extend more compassion and understanding towards others, based on her own experience of life, her relationships improved. She also started to become more self-compassionate in relation to her own body.

3. Other-to-self compassion

Have you ever tried to stop someone from hugging you because you thought you might cry if they extended kindness to you? Or have you ever tried to negate a compliment that a friend gave to you? Or have you fobbed a family member off if they tried to offer you help when you were struggling? If you've answered yes to any of these three questions, chances are that you struggle with other-to-self compassion.

Many of us experience extreme and sometimes even excruciating vulnerability in the face of accepting a kindness offered to us by someone else. We'd prefer to lend a helping hand than to accept one.

Now, think for a moment of a time that you willingly offered to help a friend in need, and they accepted your help. How did that feel? If it was a toward move for you to help this friend, in that it was freely chosen rather than foisted upon you, it's likely that you felt really good.

Now, take a moment to pause and reflect on a time when you attempted to help a friend in need who you could see was struggling and your offer of support was batted away, with your friend saying, 'Don't worry, I'm fine.' How did you feel? In this scenario, the chances are that your level of worry for your friend increased, and you probably didn't feel too good about yourself either.

Many of us have trouble accepting compassion from others. This can come down to a myriad of reasons. Our mind may generate an elaborate network of unfavourable judgements about what it means if you need to accept help from another person. It may call you weak or lazy, or deem you to be a failure. Your mind might even tell you that you'll lose friends and loved ones if you can't take care of yourself. All of these judgements make sense from an evolutionary perspective. We very much needed to be part of a group in order to survive, so our mind is constantly close to red alert for fear of being ousted from the pack.

The reality of the situation, though, is that the vast majority of us need to learn the skill of accepting compassion from others. When we learn to accept compassion and kindness from others, it bolsters our own health and psychological wellbeing, as well as to our relationships and sense of connection to others. Our loved ones will feel closer to us and comforted also when we allow them to help us.

Liliana reached a turning point when she allowed herself to listen to another person in her drama class, who had had similar experiences in the past of his mind going blank, and who empathised with her. At first, Liliana attempted to bat away her classmate's comforting actions. Her mind said that he was just saying this to make her feel better, and that he hadn't really had similar experiences. However, her curiosity was piqued enough to come back and pay more attention to the other people in the class.

When she did this, she noticed that some of the others couldn't always think of the right thing to say either. She realised that the world was not going to end if she made a mistake. The next time one of her fellow classmates opened up to her, she was more willing to listen and allow in what they had to say. Ultimately the experience of letting people empathise with her made Liliana feel more confident in her abilities because she recognised her own humanity.

TODAY'S SMALL STEP

Overcoming your compassion blocks

Take a moment to assess which of the three forms of compassion you have the most resistance to. Now sit with your legs uncrossed, feet touching the ground, and with your eyes either closed or your gaze fixed on a particular spot in the room. Sit slightly away from the back of the chair so that your back is self-supporting.

Once in this posture, take a few moments to really get grounded in your breath, scanning your body from head to toe to check in with how it feels both physically and emotionally.

You do not need to change or manipulate your breathing in any way. Nor do you need to change your body; simply notice what is going on in your body now.

You should always ground in your intention before undertaking any exercise to overcome compassion blocks, to ensure you get the most from the exercise.

* The small step you need to take now is simply a willingness to engage with the form of compassion you have chosen to work with.

* For self-to-self compassion, simply imagine extending kindness and support from yourself to yourself. This could be in the form of a kind word, or placing a hand on your heart or stomach.

Simply imagine having your own back in a difficult situation.

✳ For self-to-other compassion, simply imagine extending kindness and support to another person. Pick a person who is a little outside of your comfort zone, yet still firmly planted within your self-care zone, someone who you may have had difficulty with but don't actively dislike. Imagine giving them a kind word of support or a hug, or extending a compliment. Simply imagine giving some kindness that you would usually hold back.

✳ For other-to-self compassion, imagine allowing another person to show you kindness and support. Pick a person who is a little outside of your comfort zone, yet still firmly planted within your self-care zone, someone you wouldn't ordinarily be comfortable being vulnerable in front of. Imagine this person giving you a hug, or saying a kind word of support, or extending a compliment to you. Imagine accepting it. Simply imagine fully allowing support and kindness that you would normally bat away.

29
Writing Your Way

You don't write because you want to say something. You write
because you have something to say.
F Scott Fitzgerald

We are major advocates of writing as a small skill that the
vast majority of us could benefit from engaging in more.
There are many different things we can write about. We can
write about our struggles. We can write about what we are
grateful for. We can write about our own lives. We can write
about other people's lives. We can write about reality. We
can write about a completely fictional world that we have
created within the confines of our own minds. Spending
even a few minutes writing per day can be really helpful in
terms of your health and vitality, and your sense of creativity,
purpose and contribution.

Setting aside a small amount of time for writing each day
will help you fully integrate the Power of Small into your

life. Here are some ways that could help you to start writing towards a better life.

Track your toward and away moves

We often ask people who we are working with to set aside five minutes each day to review the 24 hours that have just gone by and the 24 hours ahead, in terms of toward and away moves.

We suggest choosing the same time every day to do this and planning it around an existing, well-established habit. This maximises your chances of sticking to this small commitment.

This small task has been transformative for many people we have worked with. Often, we find ourselves repeating the same old patterns, yet we feel powerless to know what to do with them or how to change them. Tracking your toward and away moves on a daily basis helps you to hone your perceptive skills, and see the tiny changes that could make the biggest impact. This process involves a willingness to sit with uncomfortable feelings, because most of us do not like to look at aspects of our lives that are going awry and to take responsibility for them.

Write whatever comes to mind for 15 minutes

In today's world of constant distractions, it can be extremely difficult to find any space to decipher our own thoughts and opinions. We are hearing others' thoughts and opinions 24/7, so it can be refreshing to give ourselves time and space each day to write down whatever is going through our minds.

This is a space where you can be trivial. It can include writing down things you wouldn't dream of saying for fear of hurting someone's feelings or for concern of what others might think. These 15 minutes daily are your space to air whatever is on your mind. And if the only things that are on your mind seem small, irrelevant or simply whiny, it's all good material.

Our mind is constantly judging, evaluating and comparing in any case, whether we're aware of it or not. Writing these internal experiences into the external world of the page can help us to unblinker from unwanted thoughts, see patterns that continually re-emerge, and identify what both our values and our vulnerabilities are.

Write down three small things you are grateful for and three small things you find challenging every day

Many of you will have heard that it's helpful to write down a gratitude list each day for aspects of your life that you are grateful for or appreciative of. However, if you are feeling completely overwhelmed, the prospect of writing down three things you are grateful for may be completely outside your self-care zone and could thus do more harm than good.

The Power of Small approach is all about balance. We believe that it is always best to balance acknowledging the sweet and the challenging aspects of our lives. Also, by adding the caveat that the grateful aspects and challenging aspects should be small, this helps us to release those incredibly high expectations that many of us place on ourselves, and our lives.

Through acknowledging small moments of gratitude, our awareness of what we are grateful for heightens. This could be as simple as being grateful for a smile, a good cup of coffee, or a day of sunny weather. Similarly, through acknowledging the small stressors in our lives, we validate them. We can write down that we were stuck in traffic, or got a bigger electricity bill than expected, or stubbed our toe. The research shows that unacknowledged small stressors can add up to have as big an impact as the larger stressors that most of us are far more understanding of.

Write uncensored letters (that you will not send)

Another very effective tool we have used with a number of people involves channelling unwanted emotions, such as sadness, anger, frustration and resentment, into writing uncensored letters to the person we identify as the cause of these unwanted feelings within us.

Many of us get caught in the quicksand, under the carpet and over-identifying traps around strong, intense, unwanted emotions. The process of writing down your uncensored thoughts towards this person helps you to spring those traps. You might even recognise that what you are feeling is related to another incident in your learning and life history so far.

It goes without saying that it is best not to send these uncensored letters. They are for you, and you alone.

Write a letter from your older, wiser, more compassionate self

When you are feeling very stuck in a rut and completely overwhelmed by a current life situation, it can be very useful to imagine connecting to an older, wiser, more compassionate version of yourself who has been through all that you have been through and more, and has come out the other side stronger and closer in line to their values. Write a letter to yourself from the older version of yourself, giving you the benefit of your experience and self-love. From this perspective, many more options become available to us.

Write about past challenges

Many people find it helpful to reflect and write about past challenges in their lives, such as bereavements, periods of overwhelm, separations and loss. Writing about such challenges can help us to make sense of our experiences, which can be normalising and validating for many.

    The key is that you tune in to your values and choose your toward move from that place.

Write fiction

Creative writing is a helpful process on multiple levels. Writing fiction, even if your mind tells you that you're not good enough, gives you the chance to create another world.

    Some works of fiction may be loosely centred around your own life or past challenges that you have experienced.

In this way, allowing a small amount of time each day to write fiction can really help you to process some of your own past experiences in a way that for many can feel somewhat safer. Because you are fictionalising, your experiences are one step removed, making the process more firmly planted within your self-care zone.

Sometimes an experience you witnessed, an event or episode that happened to a loved one, or something you are passionate about presents itself as the seed for a fictional project. This too can really help you identify your inner core values and vulnerabilities.

Sometimes fiction can be a science fiction, or a dystopian or fantasy world, which really allows your imagination to expand beyond the bounds of our current reality. This expansiveness can translate into an additional expansiveness in terms of your actions in your daily life.

A note about sharing your writing

Whenever you put any piece of writing out into the world for others to see, it brings the possibility of appreciation, validation, normalisation and acceptance. Unfortunately, it also brings the possibility of invalidation, hurtful comments and shaming experiences.

We are not saying this to warn you off sharing. However, we recommend practising the unblinkering strategies for unwanted thoughts, and the small strategies to spring out of emotional traps, before, during and after sharing your writing.

For many, the process of sharing writing can feel incredibly exposing and vulnerable. If this is the case for you, please know that you are not alone. If you really want to share your writing, as best you can, practise the Power of Small steps, gradually increasing how much of your writing you share and with whom.

TODAY'S SMALL STEP

Choose one writing challenge

Tune in to your values and the reason you are reading this book now. From one important value, choose which one of the writing challenges above would be the biggest toward move for you, while remaining within your self-care zone. In your small steps diary, write for ten to 15 minutes. Consider extending this to once a day for a week.

30
Short Active Reflections

*Often the moment when we most need to pause is exactly when it
feels most intolerable to do so.*
Tara Brach

In our practice we teach our clients and workshop attendees short active reflections, which they can use on a daily basis. Each short active reflection takes just five to ten minutes to do. The feedback we get from those who use these reflections on a consistent basis is that they can be really helpful in terms of gaining new perspectives.

Part of being human involves our natural propensity towards states of overwhelm, particularly when many things are happening that feel outside of our control and simply too much to handle simultaneously. Far from indicating that there's something wrong with you, feeling overwhelmed in these circumstances is just part of life.

The great news is that these short active reflections can help you to make some sense of your experience, and decipher what small skills you need to employ in the overwhelming situation you are facing. In this chapter we share five of our favourite short reflections to help you for when life feels overwhelming. You'll notice that there are some practices that are repeated in different exercises. This is deliberate. A key thing to remember about the human brain is that we often need to repeat similar processes again and again to establish them as thinking habits.

Some people prefer to listen to an audio of these instructions. We have provided an audio version of each exercise on our website.

The starting point for all short active reflections

All short active reflections will yield the best possible results if you do them while sitting in an upright and alert position. If you lie down doing these exercises, you are more likely to enter a state of day dreaming or sleep, neither of which are ideal in terms of accessing the alternative perspective that you need for the current overwhelming situation.

It's best to sit with your legs uncrossed, feet touching the ground, and with your eyes either closed or your gaze fixed on a particular spot in the room. Sit slightly away from the back of the chair so that your back is self-supporting.

Once in this posture, take a few moments to really get grounded in your breath, scanning your body from head to toe to check in with how it feels both physically and emotionally.

You do not need to change or manipulate your breathing in any way. Nor do you need to change your body; simply notice what is going on in your body now.

You should always ground in your intention before undertaking each short active reflection, to ensure you get the most from the exercise.

Different short reflections are better for different scenarios. We will help you to identify which short active reflection is best for which scenario in your life.

The serenity challenge

When to use: This exercise is ideal for situations that feel completely overwhelming. If you notice your mind and attention continually going back to a particular situation in your life, such as a difficulty in a relationship or at work, this active reflection can really help you identify which small skills you need for which parts of the current scenario.

The reflection: Having grounded yourself, as best you can identify your intention underlying this reflection. In general, we are only motivated to do the serenity challenge when we are challenged in our life.

Thinking about your current situation, what are the aspects you need to accept, which you cannot change? These aspects include your own thoughts, emotions and bodily sensations; others' thoughts, emotions, bodily sensations and actions; and your own actions in the past and in the future. Gently notice what parts of your situation right now are outside of your control.

As best you can, channel the same kind of love, caring and kindness to yourself that you would extend to a dear friend if they were going through what you are going through. You don't necessarily need to feel compassion for yourself right now. All you need is the *willingness* to imagine extending compassion towards yourself.

With the next out-breath, gently let go of this part of the exercise, taking a few mindful, connected, grounding breaths.

The second part of the serenity challenge is about having the courage to change the things that are within your power. As best you can, notice what small changes might make a positive difference to your current situation and to you right now. This may be in relation to how you respond to yourself, to your loved ones or work colleagues, or to a particular task at hand. Notice some small actions that would take courage on your part and perhaps even result in some short-term pain, yet are most likely to also bring long term gain and bring your power back.

With the next out-breath gently let go of this part of the exercise, taking a few mindful, connected, grounded breaths.

Lastly, ask for the wisdom to know the difference between the things you can and cannot change. When do you need to practise acceptance and self-compassion, and when would you benefit from courage and valued action?

Often these two are inextricably linked. In order to engage

in acceptance, we need to be courageous enough to extend compassion to ourselves, even when our minds tell us that we don't deserve it. Whenever we engage in a courageous action, we usually need to practise acceptance and self-compassion for the many self-limiting thoughts our mind may conjure up. The mind has a great tendency to be like an overprotective parent and can also be self-critical at times.

Give yourself the space to reflect on where you need to accept what you cannot change and where you need the courage to change what you can. Over time, this will give you the wisdom to know the difference.

Before you finish this exercise, it's best to think of one small action that you can apply from the exercise to get your power back. You should also choose when you will next do this short reflection. Daily practice is most likely to give you exactly what you need.

Then, when you're ready and in your own time, open your eyes and take a gentle stretch. Before standing up, take a moment to check in with how this short reflection has made you feel. Softly set an intention to act with courage and wisdom in the situation, as best you can.

5-minute commitment and confidence breakout

When to use: This short reflection is ideal when you want to create one small consistent action to break out of your comfort zone on an ongoing basis. It is also very helpful if you continuously set toward moves for yourself to engage in, yet frequently don't follow through. This practice will help you assess your confidence level from the get-go, so you can change your commitment to something more manageable, or plan to put some helpful infrastructure in place to maximise your chances of following through.

The reflection: Having grounded in your breath and body, as best as you can, ground in your intention. What would be most beneficial for you to reflect on right now, if you were to break out of your comfort zone for just five minutes a day? For some people this will be about doing more, for others it will be about doing less. Where do you think your five minutes of consistent action a day would be best spent?

Consistently engaging in toward moves that incrementally build on one another for five minutes each day is better than doing something once a week for one hour. So, without putting any pressure on yourself, try to think of one thing that you'd be willing to engage in for five minutes each day. It could be pausing. It could be doing one of the unblinkering from unwanted thoughts or springing emotional traps exercises. It could be being assertive, exercising or writing. It's up to you. What one task is likely to make the most impact on your life?

Once you have found one small action that you commit to engaging in consistently over the next week, check in with your confidence level. On a scale of one to ten, how confident are you that you'll follow through on this action? If your score is anything below an eight, maybe you need to change your goal, to do something else instead. It could be something smaller that would eventually bring you towards this five-minute action, or maybe you could put some infrastructure in place, such as a friend who checks in with you, reminders on your phone, or putting up Post-its around the house?

Even if you are at an eight or above, notice what you need to put in place to make it most likely that you'll follow through on this five minutes a day on a consistent basis. Be conscious of your typical blocks and away moves so you're more likely to notice them if they show up, and call them out for what they are. For example, some people tend to forget to engage in their toward moves amid their busy lives. In these cases, it can be helpful to use the same support mechanisms outlined above in relation to reminders or support from others.

Compassion towards what we are holding onto

When to use: This exercise is great for when you notice a lot of tension or strain on your body. It can be helpful for when your thoughts are on a constant washing machine trap of spinning around and around, to the extent that you are disconnected from important aspects of your life.

The reflection: Having grounded in your breath, as best you can, check in with your body, noticing if you are holding onto anything at this particular moment in time. Sometimes we notice we are holding onto something because we are holding some tension in our face or body.

If you're not quite sure what you're holding onto, simply notice what's been going on for you over the last week or so. Perhaps there have been some difficult situations in some area of your life, be that with family or friends, in work, health, personal growth or recreation.

At any given moment in time, pretty much all of us will be holding onto something. Sometimes it's something fairly recent. Sometimes it's something that goes back much further. As best you can, notice whatever you're holding onto right now, and in your mind's eye see how painful this thing is on a scale of one to ten, with one being not painful at all and ten excruciating

Now notice what the struggle dial is at, one being no struggle at all and ten being full-on struggle where all your time and energy is going into trying to fight against this pain. What level are you at now?

The invitation is to bring that struggle dial down a bit. It's about cultivating and connecting to the compassion you hold for people you care about in your life, noticing and imagining extending compassion to other people you care about who are in pain.

Now you are invited to place one hand on your heart and one hand on your stomach. Imagine that these hands represent compassion, whatever this means to you. All you need is the willingness to imagine extending compassion to yourself right here, right now, with all you are holding onto, just like the compassion that you imagined extending to your loved ones a few moments ago.

Stay as grounded as possible in your breathing as you extend compassion towards yourself.

Acknowledge what is outside of your control in this situation, the thoughts, the emotions, the bodily sensations, things that have happened in the past, things that will happen in the future, other people's responses and reactions. Then connect to what is within your control, extending compassion to yourself while connecting in with your values. What remains your core value, even in this challenging situation?

How would you like to see yourself responding in this and similar situations going forward? This is not an either/or scenario. You do not need to choose between extending compassion and changing what you are doing. You can do both simultaneously.

In fact, it is psychologically best for us if we extend compassion to what is outside of our control. So, try to remain compassionate, even if there's any confusion or uncertainty. Remembering that in the Power of Small, we are practising acceptance and commitment, not perfection and commitment.

It can be helpful after this exercise to either journal, if you are on your own, or speak to others who you trust.

Feeling fear of failure and rejection

When to use: Most of us want to run a mile from the unwanted internal experiences that looking at fears of failure and rejection bring up within us. If we put ourselves out there and do things that we have not done before, we will sometimes fail and we will sometimes be rejected. This reflection is helpful when you notice that you are preoccupied with fears of either failure or rejection, to the extent that you are engaging in many away moves.

The reflection: Having grounded yourself in your breath and body, notice in this moment which is a bigger fear in your life – the fear of failure, or the fear of rejection. Choose one of these to work with now, knowing that you can come back to the other at any time in the future. Gently ask yourself where this fear of failure or rejection comes from. Perhaps you heard messages from other people. Perhaps you failed at something before and were embarrassed.

You may not come up with an answer, but that's fine. The question is far more important than the answer at this time.

Gently reflect on the ways you are likely to fail or be rejected if you break out of your comfort zone and do something that makes you vulnerable to failure and/or rejection.

What might that look like? What might that feel like? Pay attention to what this would look like through your eyes, sound like through your ears, and feel like inside your body.

Identify ways you are likely to fail or be rejected if you stay within your comfort zone.

Pay attention to what this would look like through your eyes, sound like through your ears, and feel like inside your body.

Now notice which of these two options is more appealing to you. Allow yourself to contemplate a radically different way of approaching your fear of failure and rejection, a way that acknowledges your shared humanity and extends compassion towards those fears, yet doesn't hamper you or hold you back. This is an exercise that really benefits from being engaged with in the format of an active reflection. At an intellectual level, we will often go for the option of accessing the short-term gain of the relief of avoiding the possibility of rejection and failure. However, when we have guided people through this exercise one-to-one and in groups, the vast majority, when they fully connect at a heart level to the pain of staying in the comfort zone in the long term, choose the short-term discomfort over the long term discomfort.

Rewiring for the week ahead

When to use: We recommend choosing one day of the week where you consistently check in with your toward and away moves in the week gone by, and put some plans in place for the week ahead, to maximise your chances of living in line with your values. If your regular workweek is Monday to Friday, then a Sunday is an ideal time to do this short active reflection.

The reflection: Having grounded yourself in your breath and body, anchor in the present moment and look at the week ahead. There may be some things you're looking forward to. There may also be challenges ahead.

Now, reflect on any unwanted emotions around what's happening in the week ahead. Practise whatever acceptance and compassion strategies work best for you. It could be placing a hand, which represents compassion, on the part of your body where you feel this unwanted emotion most intensely. It could be breathing into and out from the emotion. It could be experimenting with greeting this unwanted emotion with the words and energy of 'yes', allowing rather than avoiding. Your response might be as simple as internally saying, 'It's okay for me to feel this way.' There's no right or wrong way to practise acceptance and compassion, it's just about finding what works for you.

Now gently take a look at your unwanted emotions from another perspective, from that of somebody you see as wise. It could be someone you know or perhaps someone you have never met, yet look up to. Simply imagine looking at your current situation from their perspective.

Connect in to the words you would use to describe yourself and your actions over the next week.

Gently notice what small actions you need to engage in, in order to live in line with your values. Reflect on Hyrum W Smith's words: 'The secret to achieving inner peace lies in understanding our inner core values – those things in our lives that are most important to us – and then seeing that they are reflected in the daily events of our daily lives.'

Rest in the knowledge that you can come back and do this reflection as many times as you need to over the next week.

TODAY'S SMALL STEP

Choose one short active reflection

Choose the short active reflection that you believe will be most beneficial to you in your life right now. Commit to doing this small active reflection at least three times, either daily or weekly depending on the reflection. Make some observations in your small steps diary around what you notice.

31
Planning Before and Responding After

Trust only movement. Life happens at the level of events, not of words. Trust movement. Alfred Adler

There is a key message that permeates the Power of Small: let your experiences – rather than what your mind tells you – be your guide. Your mind will tell you that you can and can't, should and shouldn't do all kinds of things. However, it is only through small, incremental, consistent actions that your life will change in meaningful directions.

The fact that you're reading this shows that you want to make some changes in your life, and you'd prefer to sustain those changes in the long term, rather than starting off all guns blazing only to find that what you've started can't be kept up. To give you the best possible chance of achieving longevity from the small strategies you adopt from this book, we'd like to introduce you to the importance of planning before and responding after.

The importance of planning before

The various different aspects of your environment and your life before you plan to take your small action are very important. Some aspects of your daily life and practice will make you more likely to engage in a small action, while some will make you less likely.

We've outlined a range of small skills in this book so far, along with other initiatives, such as sticking to an ongoing commitment of writing, exercising or engaging in reflections. If you *plan ahead* and use a combination of these before a foreseeable overwhelming event or circumstance in your life, such as changing jobs or navigating a challenging family situation, you will greatly increase your chances of following through. Not only that, but you will be creating and maintaining long term sustainable changes in your life. Our brains need practice and repetition to lock in new patterns of behaviour.

When you go about your life in a haphazard way, hoping for the best and only using the small skills when things have already gone awry, you have less chance of achieving this long term sustainable change. It is obviously important to practise your small skills after a challenging situation, yet through combining planning ahead and reassessing afterwards, you will put yourself in a very powerful position indeed. Read back on the skills outlined in this part of the book to assess in advance which of them might be most beneficial to you in bolstering your chances of following through.

Here are some small skills that you can engage in ahead of time:

* Unblinkering strategies for unwanted thoughts about a situation or event

* Springing emotional traps for unwanted emotions grounded in fear

* Writing to help you identify your patterns

* Small active reflections to establish what is inside and outside of your control

* Anchoring in your values daily for motivation

Any, and all, of these small skills, if practised for as little as a few minutes a day, will help you to consistently change your life in incremental and sustainable ways.

Responding after

The Power of Small skills not only need to be consistently practised, but you will benefit from also developing the ability to monitor the consequences of your actions.

What you do after consciously making a toward or away move makes a huge difference. Do you take time to acknowledge and assess your actions after the fact? Doing so will greatly help you to develop a clear idea of which of your past actions have helped you and which actions have hindered you.

If you engaged in a toward move, take a moment to

acknowledge this. Reflect on the impact this has had on you in line with your values. Also, acknowledge the cumulative effect that such toward moves could amount to over time.

What do you do after you engage in an away move?

Many of our natural tendencies involve either burying our heads in the sand or getting caught in the loop of a shame cycle. When we bury our heads in the sand, we do not learn what we need to learn from the situation, and as a result most of us repeat the same small away moves again and again until they become big away moves and big problems.

When we go into a shame cycle, many of us get caught up in the washing machine trap of reliving the same away move again and again, to the extent that we become so blinkered by our away moves and our unhelpful self-evaluations that we miss out on opportunities to learn and grow. As a result, we often end up repeating the same away moves and further reinforcing the same cycle.

It may seem counterintuitive, and our mind might tell us that it's self-indulgent, yet the reality is that most of us need a good, healthy dose of self-compassion when we have engaged in an away move. Self-compassion after an away move does not involve minimising the impact of the away move through pretending that it doesn't matter. Self-compassion acknowledges the impact of the away move in our lives and on ourselves.

Self-compassion also begs us to treat ourselves in a kind and caring manner, while also doing something in the moment that will truly benefit our future self. In this way, engaging in one small toward move in the aftermath of an away move, really helps to bolster our chances of learning lessons from our away move and firmly moving back towards our values, one small step at a time.

In a sense, planning before and responding after are two sides of the same coin, as one action is always preceding another in a continuous stream, so we must be as consistent as we can in monitoring our actions, before and after. If we take our eyes off the prize of having a life worth fighting for, there will be major consequences, both wanted, in terms of short-term gain, and unwanted, in terms of long term pain.

TODAY'S SMALL STEP

Your optimum planning before and responding after small actions

This part of the book has given you many small skills, exercises and reflections to help you gently move towards a life worth living. It's a lot to take in, we know, but if you use it as a reference tool, along with what you've already built up in your small steps diary, you can easily bring these skills and exercises into your everyday life.

For now, take a little time to scan back through this whole section, marking the pages, skills and exercises that stand out for you.

Now pick one or two before actions that you will put in place in advance of potentially overwhelming situations in your life. Write these down under the heading 'Planning Before' in your small steps diary, and refer to them when you know you are heading towards a situation where they will be needed.

Similarly, pick one or two 'Responding After' actions that you will mark down in your diary, to refer to when you have either made toward or away moves in your life, and are conscious of them. Make it a habit to refer to these actions when you know what moves you have made.

Part Four

Make the Power of Small a Way of Life

32
Small Takeaways

Between stimulus and response there is a space. In that space is our power to choose our response. In our response lies our growth and our freedom. Viktor E Frankl

The Power of Small way of living is not a nice, neat, before-and-after process. Rather it is a conscious way of responding that you will need to return to time and again. The path forward from here will shift and change as you navigate the many opportunities and challenges, both big and small, that life presents you with.

We have seen it many times with our clients that initially they fully embody the skills and principles outlined in this book. Then at some point, sooner or later, they forget about the skills they've built up, or they neglect to practise them on an ongoing basis, believing they don't need them anymore.

This is part of human nature. None of us are perfect and

we all let go of skills and strategies, even when they are in our own best interest. We encourage you to stay connected to the Power of Small community either through social media or our website. We want to give you the best possible chance of sustaining your small changes in an incremental and consistent manner, to help you get the best possible outcomes in your life.

This chapter will outline some of the small takeaways and nuggets that you can return to when you become lost in a sea of overwhelm and aren't quite sure where to start.

We recommend looking through the nine takeaways in this chapter and then coming back to the one that resonates most, reading this part alone and following through on the associated practice. This will be far more helpful to you than reading the whole chapter without application.

Engaging in one small section in a fully connected way is better than reading a large chunk of text without applying the small skills.

NINE TAKEAWAYS

1. Knowing that no matter how overwhelmed you are, there is always one small toward move you can make

We've explored how values are not something you can just reach out and grab directly. You do, however, have it within your power to ground and centre your actions in life so that, as best you can at any given moment, you are effectively poised to step towards those values. We highly recommend tuning in to your values each and every day. The more you do this, the more anchored and grounded you will become in your life.

When you are clear in terms of what is important to you, what you want to stand for and how you want to be remembered, you will find it far easier to choose which small actions to engage in and which actions to let go. The reality is that when we are feeling overwhelmed, we are often engaging in some actions that are in line with our values, and some, maybe habitual, actions that are not.

Your mind has evolved to be a bit of a spoilsport, always honing in on the unhelpful aspects of your life. As we have learned, it is simply doing all it can to help you avoid danger, to keep you alive. However, in this modern world our brains are in overdrive, with constant access to external distractions. It is totally natural that you would become overwhelmed by the sensory overload of all that is going on, both inside yourself and outside. However, you always have the power to choose one small action that will alter the course of your life and your reality.

A small moments practice: Take a few moments to anchor in your breath and breathing. Tune in to your body. Notice any tension or strain you might be carrying outside of your conscious awareness. Very deliberately anchor in your values. From this grounded stance, choose just one small action to engage in right now that will help bring you closer to who and where you truly want to be.

2. Knowing that seemingly insignificant things can have significant consequences for your life

In the modern world, we are constantly being spoon-fed the idea that bigger is better. Turn on your TV, smartphone or computer and you will be bombarded by images of people who our society deems 'successful', whatever that actually means. It is so easy to get caught up in the big promises, big disappointment trap.

The Power of Small approach advocates gradual exposure, or taking baby steps. You simply need to go one level further outside your comfort zone as it expands on an ongoing basis. This is akin to levels of a video game, which progress in difficulty as you proceed, but which always have a pay-off. The power of cumulative incremental effects is clearly seen in the ancient fable of Rani, as told in the children's book, *One Grain of Rice.*

> *There once was a powerful raja who presented*
> *himself as wise and fair, but each year he kept*
> *all of his people's rice to himself. Eventually a*
> *famine hit the land and the raja, still refusing to*
> *share the rice out among the people, caused mass*
> *starvation of his people.*
>
> *A village girl named Rani came up with a clever*
> *plan. She performed a good deed for the raja,*
> *in return for which he granted her anything her*

heart desired. She asked for just one grain of rice, to be doubled each and every day for the total duration of 30 days. The raja laughed mockingly, but he granted Rani her seemingly modest wish. She received one grain of rice on the first day, two on the second day, four grains on the third day, and so on.

On the ninth day Rani was presented with 256 grains of rice, enough for only a small handful. On the thirteenth day she received enough to fill a bowl. Following this, eight deer were required to manage the load of the rice amassed on the twenty-fourth day, as the grains of rice exponentially grew in number. Eventually on the thirtieth and final day, 256 elephants were gathered from all across the province to carry the burden of full bags of rice from the last of the four royal storehouses, a total of 536,870,912 grains of rice.

In total, over the 30 days, Rani received more than one billion grains of rice. She was able to distribute the rice to feed her fellow villagers, and even the nearby animals.

Incremental actions towards longer-lasting change:
Grounded in your values, choose one change you want to
make. Write down in your small steps diary whatever it is
you wish to work towards, for example cultivating a loving
relationship with someone, focusing on a more healthy diet,
or going on a much-needed break for some R&R.

Now write down one small tangible action you are willing
to take today, and each day for a predetermined period of
time. For instance, one single push-up today, plus one more
tomorrow, plus one more the next day, and in one month
you'll be doing 30 each day. One less gram of fat in your diet
today, plus one less again tomorrow and you will be ingesting
14 fewer grams in two weeks. Saving one euro today for that
break away, plus one more than that again tomorrow, and
one more than that again the following day for as long as
you can will build up a substantial holiday fund.

3. Focusing on what you do have control over

Nowadays, houses, apartments and office buildings need
to be assessed to see how energy efficient they are. There
are minimal standards in place to ensure that buildings
conserve their energy. However, few of us carry out a similar
assessment on ourselves to recognise where we are losing
our energy, and how we might conserve it.

We waste huge amounts of time and energy in trying
to control things that we simply cannot, for example; our
pasts and our futures, our internal worlds, and other people.

Meanwhile, we lose contact and connection with, and control over, the aspects of our lives that we can do something about – our values, attitudes and actions right this very moment.

A small practice to conserve your energy and power: Whenever you notice yourself exhausted and overwhelmed, it can be helpful to do an energy assessment. Take a few moments to drop anchor into your breath and body, exactly as they are. Tune in to how much of your time and energy is being wasted trying to control the aspects of your life that are essentially out of your control – namely attempting to control your unwanted internal experiences, other people, your past or your future.

Then, as best you can, assess how much of your time and energy is being wisely invested in the aspects of your life that are within your control – namely your values, attitudes and actions right this moment.

If you notice that you are draining your power, acknowledge this as compassionately as possible. This is part of being human. Our desire to control and predict is part of our evolutionary hardwiring. Consciously choose some skills from your Power of Small toolkit that you can apply for the aspects that are outside of your control. Most importantly, choose one or two small actions that are within your control. This will help you to regain a sense of influence in your own life.

4. Not mistaking balance for safety

If I want to be secure, that is, protected from the flux of life, I
am wanting to be separate from life. Yet it is this very sense of
separateness which makes me
feel insecure. Alan Watts

The idea that everything should be steady and secure is not balance. This is a notion that we may have systematically constructed and bought into as a society, but the truth is that to take any step or move in any direction, we must momentarily surrender our balance. This is a necessary part of the progress of growth and movement.

Like happiness or contentment, balance is not a stable state that we can maintain all of the time. Even the action of walking has been described as a continual process of losing and regaining balance. The trick is to practise the skills that will increase your ability to recompose yourself after you lose your balance.

From the Power of Small perspective, you need both balance and imbalance. You need to be willing to engage in toward moves, even when they bring up discomfort. Just as importantly, you need to engage in self-care and nourishing actions. Balancing both movement and stillness will give you the best chance of lasting and meaningful changes in the long term. As with most things in life, we need balance in moderation.

A balancing–rebalancing practice: Drop anchor into this present moment and whatever is going on for you right now. Notice the areas that need more balance. These will generally be the areas where you tend to operate at excessive levels, the places in your life where you are in do-do, go-go mode. Choose one small self-caring action that would be nurturing and nourishing, to bring you closer towards balance and operating at a level that has the best chances of longevity.

Now, also notice the areas in your life where you need some imbalance. Perhaps you under stretch yourself in these areas, where you are caught in your comfort zone, staying perpetually in a place that is unfulfilling, fearful of stretching beyond this. This is where you need some imbalance. You need to shake things up a bit to gain some meaningful change. Choose one small action to move towards where you want to be, which will inevitably bring some imbalance.

Remember, balance can only be regained from imbalance.

5. Knowing the difference between responding and reacting

Most of us get caught up in cycles of reactivity. When we react, we rarely make conscious decisions about how we will respond. Rather, our actions are on autopilot. In this mode, we are frequently driven by our unwanted thoughts, emotions and physical sensations, and our desire to quench and quell such unwanted internal experiences. When certain buttons are pressed or boundaries are ignored or violated, our red alert system will activate. From this place, more often than not, we react. And the vast majority of these reactions are away moves.

Small survival guide practice: If you know that you are entering a situation or environment where your red alert system is likely to be activated, it can be extremely helpful to review, revise and practise the small skills you have learned and marked throughout this book. Planning ahead, and having tried and tested skills at your fingertips, will increase your chances of responding in a way that is aligned with your values.

Often when we react, we can go into a continued spiral of reactivity. This is where we dig ourselves deeper and deeper into an already unwanted situation and set of responses. As soon as you notice that you are in a spiral of reactivity, you can do something about it. It is never too late to start practising your small skills. Every reaction digs you further into the hole and further away from who and where you want to be. Every conscious response in line with your values helps bring you back closer to who and where you want to be.

6. Taking time to respond to the world

Our technologically-driven cultural context may demand our attention and immediate reactions to fast-paced content, but you do not need to be online and available to respond 24/7. You also do not have to respond the moment you see something.

Research is very clear that after a couple of weeks of working 60-plus-hours, people are no more effective than those who are working 40-hour weeks. A similar process is at play in terms of how many hours we are 'on' being highly responsive to social media, email and messaging apps. The quality of connections is bound to suffer. There's a growing body of research to support this, along with other harmful effects of our increasing attachment to technology.

Rather than focusing on quantity and speed of response, experiment with changing your focus to the quality of responses.T his is particularly important if you receive information that is somewhat triggering for you and leads to feelings of anger, frustration and resentment.

It is generally an away move to respond in a way that completely invalidates your own feelings. However, it is also generally an away move to respond in a way that is totally fuelled by these feelings and your desire to alleviate them. Responses, or more accurately reactions, from this place may very well contain some important and valid pieces of information. However, when you react from a place of anger, frustration or resentment, many of your comments will be taken far less seriously. It is best to carefully compose a response from a place of awareness, courage and compassion in equal measure.

A turning your focus inwards practice: When you receive a difficult email, app message or social media reply, pause and take a moment or two to connect to yourself and your values in response to the information you're being presented with. Give yourself some wiggle room to stop and shift your attention inwards to how you really feel about the message you have just received.

Bring awareness to the fullness of your experience. Have the courage to express to yourself in the form of reflection or writing, for your own eyes only, how you feel. Bring compassion first for yourself in relation to whatever response you are having. Then bring compassion to the other person or parties involved. This doesn't mean that you need to like, love or want them, or like how they are responding. It simply involves taking a moment to acknowledge the common humanity that you share with them.

Once you have reached a place of awareness, courage and compassion in equal measure, craft a reply. If you can, run the reply by someone who you trust to be wise and able to give you sound guidance.

7. Knowing how to be flexible when it comes to your values

It can be helpful to think of your values as a set of dice. Just like a dice is multi-faceted, so too are your values. For example, during the time of writing this book, the value of writing a book that we wish we could have read when each of us struggled most with anxiety and depression, came to the forefront. As a result, we saw family and friends less than we would do normally.

It wasn't that our families or friends were less important

to us; it was simply a case of realising that writing this book needed to be done within a certain timeframe. While writing our book, there were times when our families really needed us, due to ill health. At these points, the caring for loved ones value came to the forefront. We didn't care any less about this book, it was simply a matter of urgency. There were also times when we needed to tend to our own self-care by nurturing and nourishing our own needs, so that we could write more effectively. This was another side of the dice.

What we're aiming for is flexibility. Even though the idea is to let your values guide your actions, just like with anything else, it becomes problematic when you cling too tightly to one value, even when the present moment demands an alternative response. It's times like this when it is helpful to honestly ask yourself if you're really being true to your values, or perhaps acting out of wilfulness.

A values practice in relation to self: Thinking about the dice that represents your values, tune in to what aspects of your life are most important to you. Then tune in to which value is most important in this present moment. It does not mean that this value is more important than all the others on an ongoing basis, although this may be the case. It simply means that you are making an active choice in terms of which action to engage in that's in line with your overall values, while being in line with your moment-to-moment values at the same time.

A values practice in relation to others: Inevitably, sometimes our core values will conflict with someone else's. In these situations, it will help if you can connect with awareness, courage and compassion in relation to your own values and those of the other person. You do not have to agree with everything the other believes or says. However, it will most likely help if you can tune in to your inner wisdom and connect to what is important in relation to this person in the here and now.

8. Choosing discomfort over resentment

Dr Brené Brown coined the phrase, 'Choose discomfort over resentment.' It is a phrase that can really pay dividends in your life.

Often, we trap ourselves with automatic responses to requests or comments from others – we say yes without really thinking, and when our minds catch up to the difficult consequences of our action, we kick ourselves for saying yes in the first place. When our problem-solving mode can't work out a way to get us out of what we've just committed to, we can fall into resentment, unhelpful self-talk and wilfulness. On the flipside, sometimes we would love to say yes to something, yet we say no because we become blinkered by the thought that we 'don't have enough time', or that we are 'too busy' and that whatever we've been asked to do is frivolous in some way.

For example, Pauline is a working mother of three. She often feels torn between her different roles, and strives to do her best in all areas of her life. She often chooses resentment over discomfort, such as when she's asked to do extra work at the weekend. Feeling the pressure to appear just as hardworking as any of her colleagues who don't have children, she frequently says yes to her manager, yet then finds herself increasingly resentful over the weekend, as her husband goes to the cinema with their children while she stays at home in front of her computer screen.

Pauline starts to notice increasingly unwanted thoughts and emotions towards her manager for her perceived insensitivity, and she finds herself snapping at the children in moments of exhaustion. When Pauline's friends ask her to go on a girls' night out, she would love to go; however, she feels so guilty about bringing work home, yet again, that she becomes blinkered by the thought that she couldn't possibly go on a night out. So, she says no. And then she notices increasing resentment building up again as she sees her friends post photos up on Facebook looking like they are having the time of their lives.

In order for Pauline to choose discomfort over resentment, she would need to set limits with her manager. For Pauline, the toward move she engaged in was signifying that she would only work one weekend in the month, and that this would need to be predetermined in advance. This brought up a lot of discomfort for Pauline, as she had anxiety about how her manager would react. Obviously, her manager would have preferred if Pauline had continued to work most weekends, and she did attempt to lure Pauline back into her previous weekend working ways a few times in the first couple of months.

Ultimately, though, Pauline's manager respected her decision and there weren't any adverse consequences. Interestingly – and this is in line with research on productivity – after a couple of weeks of Pauline working fewer evenings and weekends, her creativity and productivity increased, and she managed to cover much more work in the time that she was in work. She felt more refreshed returning to work on a Monday after having a weekend with her family, and at least one Saturday night out with her friends each month. The cost of the discomfort in the short term was more than worth it for the reduction in resentment in the long term.

A choosing discomfort over resentment practice: Take a moment to pause and reflect on the areas in your life where you choose resentment over discomfort in your relationships with others. Connect at a very real and deep level to the *benefits* of choosing resentment over discomfort for you and your relationships. Now, also connect at a very real and deep level to the costs of choosing resentment over discomfort.

Very often the costs outweigh the benefits. Many of us have been raised in a culture of putting others' needs before our own. Sometimes this is helpful and even necessary. However, not always. It is all about balance, and if you constantly place the needs of others before your own, you will most likely suffer the consequences that derive from lack of self-care.

Give yourself a couple of minutes in silence to let this mantra of *choosing discomfort over resentment* percolate. Then choose one small action that you will engage in that will clearly show that you are living this mantra. As best you can, choose something that is outside of your comfort zone, yet nestled firmly within your self-care zone.

9. Not letting the reality gap swallow you up

At any given moment in time, we will have at least a few reality gaps in our lives. This is a natural part of living in the modern world, where our seeming lack can feel like it's slapping us on the face anytime we take a look at what everyone else is up to. Sometimes, the reality gap between our ideal life and our current life feels like a chasm.

There will always be others who are doing more than us, have more than us, and seem to have their life together more than us. Many of us are – constantly as best selling author, Steven Furtick, frames it – comparing our behind-the-scenes to everyone else's highlight reel.

It never ceases to amaze us how often our clients are surprised to realise that other people's realities do not resemble so closely the carefully curated and manicured images that they choose to share on social media.

It can be helpful to let go of expectations and outcomes and instead engage in the process, one small step at a time. Realising that there will always be a gap, and that this is simply part of the price of admission for humanity, can be incredibly liberating.

For example, Lee and Sam are two friends who are both in their 40s and are feeling a reality gap in that neither of them yet own their own home.

Doing the practice outlined below, Lee realised that owning a home is very important to him; also that he very often spends money frivolously on things that don't really give him much joy, or add anything meaningful to his life. For example, he has several subscriptions that he doesn't even use.

Lee's first step was to spend 15 minutes a day going through subscriptions and making a choice to let them go if they were an away move for him. After Lee did this, he then spent five to ten minutes a day logging his spending, and acknowledging which spending was toward and which was away. Within the first month, Lee had saved €400. He started putting these little chunks of money away each day to bridge his reality gap.

Sam, on the other hand, after doing the reality gap practice, realised that she was feeling pressure because her friends had bought homes, and her family had made a number of off-hand comments about her need to buy a home sooner rather than later.

Through the practice, Sam realised that while she wanted to live somewhere she liked, buying a home wasn't an urgent priority for her right now. As she anchored in her values, she realised that saving for a three-month trip to South America that she'd always dreamt of would be more in line with her true values-guided reality gap, rather than the socially enforced reality gap that she had originally been preoccupied with. She still did a similar awareness of her spending. However, unlike Lee, she happily spent money on trips as this was in line with her values.

A bridging the reality gap practice: Take out your small steps diary. Before you start writing, give yourself a few moments of stillness to reacquaint yourself with how you are in this moment. Do a quick scan of your thoughts, emotions and bodily sensations. Then, anchor in your breath and body.

From this place of embodiment, take a few minutes to recognise and acknowledge the reality gaps that exist in your life. These are any areas where your reality does not match the experiences you wish you had. As best you can, recognise that reality gaps are a non-negotiable part of being human. Simply acknowledge whether these reality gaps bother you because you think that you *should* be different, or whether they are a signal of something that truly matters to you.

If the pain around a reality gap is based on shoulds and societal expectations, practise your unblinkering and springing emotional traps skills. If this reality gap highlights something that truly matters, give yourself compassion for the pain you are experiencing and find one small action that you can engage in immediately to begin the process of bridging the gap.

TODAY'S SMALL STEP

Read and follow through on one takeaway

As best you can, resisting the urge to read all the takeaways and apply none of the practices, really tune in to yourself and your unmet needs in this present moment. Read and follow through on the takeaway and practice that you most need in order to cultivate a compassionate relationship with yourself. Remember, true compassion involves doing something today that your future self will thank you for.

33
FUEL Yourself

Many people die with their music still in them. Why is this so? Too often it is because they are always getting ready to live. Before they know it, time runs out. Oliver Wendell Holmes

Living the life of your dreams is not just for extraordinary people who master a specific set of skills. And it does not have to comprise what a marketer, blogger, parent, or your friends tell you what you *should* want from life. You have the tools and the skills at your fingertips to live a life that is rich, fulfilling and meaningful to you, and you alone. You get to choose the course of your life.

Our aim is always to help you expand your life where it matters most. We hope you have learned the flexibility to come back to what is important, especially when you get knocked off track; and we hope that you will continue to apply what you have learned to your life. Through the skills taught in this book, you can regain balance in the face of inevitable setbacks. The key to longevity lies in sustaining and nourishing your life daily and consistently.

Please remember:

1. Anything worth doing is worth doing consistently, while refining what you do and don't do in line with whether it is pragmatic.

2. Compassionately look back on what you've achieved since starting this book.

3. It is human nature to go off track, but you have set the context for long term meaningful change that you can come back to whenever you've wandered off course.

FUEL

We have created a four-step process that you can return to at any time when you're feeling overwhelmed or simply adrift out at sea. As you continue forwards on your Power of Small path, you will inevitably need FUEL in order to renavigate and reorient yourself back towards what matters, in line with your values.

F – Find the most important values in the present moment.

U – Unblinker from your self-limiting thoughts and stories.

E – Expand to make room for unwanted and uncomfortable emotions.

L – Look after yourself with compassion.

This four-step process will help you to stay within your limits by honouring your own needs for love and care as you would for someone you love. Concentrate on the things you do have control over and take responsibility for the actions you choose to take.

Take responsibility for your life

Dr Albert Ellis, psychologist and developer of rational emotive behaviour therapy (REBT), proposed that the best years of our lives are the ones in which we realise our problems are our own: when we stop blaming others and decide that we have the power to own our own responses.

We believe that each of us needs to be aware of the areas in which we are taking under-responsibility by blaming our life circumstances on others. We equally need to be aware of our tendency to pendulum-swing into over-responsibility, when we attempt to control and assume responsibility for aspects of our lives that are outside of our control, namely our internal experiences, our past, our future and other people.

We invite you to engage in three small, yet powerful, actions on an ongoing basis.

1. Expose yourself to taking risks of failure, rejection

and getting it wrong, when these same actions are moves that will bring you closer to a life aligned with your values.

2. Be kind and compassionate to yourself (and others) when you do engage in these actions, and also when you don't.

3. Remember that true compassion is doing something that will benefit future you.

TODAY'S SMALL STEP

FUEL yourself

Practise this four-step process to FUEL yourself, as outlined above. Track what you notice while doing this exercise in your small steps diary.

Epilogue
A Letter from Us to You

Wanderer, worshipper, lover of leaving. It doesn't matter.
Ours is not a caravan of despair.
Come, even if you have broken your vow
a thousand times.
Come, yet again, come, come.
Rumi

When we run groups and workshops, one of the final small tasks we often invite people to do is to write a letter to the other members of the group and themselves. The idea is that this letter is something that the members of the group can come back to when they're feeling overwhelmed, down or anxious.

There isn't a right or wrong way to write this letter. The requirement is to write from your heart in a compassionate, supportive and kind way, offering any nuggets of guidance that you have, which might be helpful when someone is going through a challenging time. We also ask each person to write a letter to themselves from their older, wiser, more compassionate self, to help them through this challenging time. This is a really nice way to bring all the small skills together.

Do the best you can until you know better. Then when you know better, do better.

Maya Angelou

Our letter to you for when times are tough:

Dear reader

If you're reading this, chances are that you are going through a challenging time. We want you to know and remember that to struggle is a perfectly natural part of living a human life. Even with the best of intentions and even when you engage in lots of toward moves, life will still throw you curveballs.

We have had plenty of curveballs in our own lives. We can relate to how overwhelming and insurmountable these can feel at the time. Please know that you are not alone. We get it. And so do many others. The tough thing is that many people won't share when they're struggling, so sometimes you can feel like you're struggling and suffering alone. It's very easy to get blinkered by the thought that there's something wrong with you.

When lots of things go awry all at once, it can feel impossible to know where you should even start. As best you can, drop an anchor into your values. Ask yourself some questions to assess what words you would like to use to describe yourself and how you would like to be remembered. These words and characteristics will give you very strong clues as to what would be toward moves for you in this present challenge.

Remember that you can reacquaint yourself with any, and all, of the small skills you've gained here, whenever you need them. Sometimes when you are especially overwhelmed, it can feel like you've forgotten them altogether. However, luckily for you, the skills are still inside you – they can't be deleted. There just might be a few layers of dust on top of them.

The moment you stop, and anchor in your breath and values, you are already dusting them off.

Never forget: there is always one small thing that you can do, in the now, to help. Just start by anchoring in your breath and values and it will become clear. It might be as small as putting on the kettle, when you didn't feel you could move from the bed. Or reaching out to a friend, when you feel most like isolating yourself. Sit with the discomfort, then take the small action.

After you've engaged in this, assess whether this action brings you closer to who and where you want to be or further away.

Either way, you will learn something. And either way, you will know better what next step to take.

With warmest wishes in this moment and all the small moments,

Aisling & Trish

A thousand-mile journey
begins with a single step.
Lao Tzu

TODAY'S SMALL STEP

Write a letter from your older, wiser, more compassionate self for challenging times

With our letter to you as a guide, take some time to reflect on what your older, wiser, more compassionate self would offer you in the form of a letter of support.

Often retrospective thinking is 20/20 vision. Give yourself a chance to write any quotes, poems, sayings or general guidance that would be helpful in challenging times. If you are willing, it can be incredibly helpful to let a dear friend know about this letter so they can remind you to read it when you need it most.

Acknowledgements

While this book may be called *The Power of Small*, it has by no means been a small feat. We have been blessed to have the support of many, many people around the world, and we would like to take the opportunity to thank them now.

Thank you to Ciara Considine, our editor, who read the original article in *The Irish Times* on 5-minute breakouts, and believed in the concept of small and the need for this book at this time. Thanks also to Joanna Smith, and the rest of the Hachette Ireland team for their help and support throughout this process.

Thank you to Roisin Ingle, who published the first article about 5-minute breakouts in *The Irish Times*, which generated widespread interest in the concept of small, and encouraged us to distil the many small skills and strategies that we have been offering for years into the form of a book.

There have been many cheerleaders and major supporters of our work along the way. Sam Kelly, otherwise known as

Tweeting Goddess, Helena Gilhooly and all the members of Women's Inspire Network have been very supportive of us on Twitter and throughout social media. The Professional Speakers Association have provided invaluable feedback in terms of how to communicate our messages out to as many people as possible. Thank you to Victoria Mary Clarke and Tara Gilleece who both helped us to prepare for the media to share our ideas with as many people as possible. Fellow psychologist Malie Coyne has also been a major supporter and cheerleader of our work, thank you.

We feel so blessed and fortunate to be part of the Association for Contextual Behavioural Science, the international organisation for acceptance and commitment therapy (ACT). The organisation, and the trainers within it, provided so many rich opportunities to learn, teach and collaborate the whole world over. So many of the small skills in this book are inspired by the work of fellow trainers. Benji Schoendorff introduced us to the concept of the self-care zone, which has become pivotal in the Power of Small approach. Robyn Walser, and Matthieu and Jennifer Villatte taught us so much about coherent and incoherent narratives and stories.

The functional analytic psychotherapy (FAP) community have provided us with a lot of awareness, courage and love through the years. We are grateful for our many FAP friends and their contributions in our lives. Mavis Tsai, one of the co-founders of FAP, has been a particularly strong influence.

Thank you to the Act Now Purposeful Living team, in

particular Tracy Quinn and JoJo Shiadool, who have helped us extensively over the last number of years.

There were a number of people who reviewed our manuscript and gave us feedback throughout this process. We are so grateful to Aoife Herrity, Anne Marie Graham, Finola Howard, Kirk Strosahl, Louise McHugh, Michael Sinclair, Rick Doody, Rosalind Healy and Russ Harris.

We'd like to thank Camille Hayes for fantastic writing guidance and support along the way.

We are very grateful to and for the Irish Writers Centre – a fantastic resource and support for all aspiring Irish writers. Much of the early drafts of *The Power of Small* were written within the Irish Writers Centre.

Brian Finnegan provided invaluable input in terms of how to structure and best present the concepts within *The Power of Small*, for which we are incredibly grateful.

A massive thank you goes to Olivia O'Leary, who took time amidst her incredibly busy schedule to read our manuscript and provide such a beautiful and thoughtful foreword to our book. We are so very appreciative of this.

Thank you to all the amazing people around the world who took time out of their busy lives to review and endorse our book in such genuine and heartfelt ways – Dennis Tirch, Jennifer O'Connell, Kirk Strosahl, Laura Silberstein-Tirch, Lisa Coyne, Mary Welford, Michael Sinclair, Niall Breslin, Ruth Scott, Russ Harris and Steven C Hayes.

Our family and close friends have been incredibly supportive throughout the process of writing. There were very many things and people that we needed to say no to in order to get this book completed, and we are extremely grateful to all of you for your understanding. We are particularly grateful to our immediate and extended families and to our closest friends, who are like our chosen extended family.

We are so grateful for our furry babies – Loki, who passed during the process of writing this book; Shanti, Leia and Luna. You four have given us an abundance of snuggles and love. You have taught us how to stay grounded in the present moment, and have let us know when we've been sitting in front of the computer for too long.

We thank you, dear reader, for your willingness to read and implement this book, at this moment in time.

Last, but certainly not least, we owe a massive debt of gratitude to our many clients, and workshop and group attendees, who constantly gave us feedback and asked us questions, to help us refine this model further and further. This book was shaped by your input and it is for you. We hope that it will serve as a constant guide that you can return to again and again.

Aisling and Trish are now leading Power of Small workshops for those who want some additional support in making tiny but powerful changes when everything feels too much in their daily lives. For more information on in-person Power of Small workshops, online Power of Small courses, as well as access to free resources to accompany this book, check out www.mypowerofsmall.com